CAMBRIDGE LIBRARY COLLECTION

Books of enduring scholarly value

History

The books reissued in this series include accounts of historical events and movements by eye-witnesses and contemporaries, as well as landmark studies that assembled significant source materials or developed new historiographical methods. The series includes work in social, political and military history on a wide range of periods and regions, giving modern scholars ready access to influential publications of the past.

Report of the Lords of the Privy Council on Commerce and Navigation

The Committee was commissioned to report on the state of trade between Britain and America after the United States Congress had passed legislation imposing duties and restrictions on imports in 1789. Merchants and ship owners in the major British ports and British consuls in America were sent questionnaires on the effects of such levies. The committee made its report in 1791, and began by summarising the situation since Britain had acknowledged American independence in 1783, and how independence had affected trade, including that involving slaves, between the two countries. The decline in British exports to the United States had been offset by exports to Canada and the West Indies. Overall, the balance of trade was in Britain's favour, but the continuing prosperity of the British West Indian colonies was seen as depending almost entirely on their slave-based economy, and abolition was therefore not believed to be an option.

Cambridge University Press has long been a pioneer in the reissuing of out-of-print titles from its own backlist, producing digital reprints of books that are still sought after by scholars and students but could not be reprinted economically using traditional technology. The Cambridge Library Collection extends this activity to a wider range of books which are still of importance to researchers and professionals, either for the source material they contain, or as landmarks in the history of their academic discipline.

Drawing from the world-renowned collections in the Cambridge University Library, and guided by the advice of experts in each subject area, Cambridge University Press is using state-of-the-art scanning machines in its own Printing House to capture the content of each book selected for inclusion. The files are processed to give a consistently clear, crisp image, and the books finished to the high quality standard for which the Press is recognised around the world. The latest print-on-demand technology ensures that the books will remain available indefinitely, and that orders for single or multiple copies can quickly be supplied.

The Cambridge Library Collection will bring back to life books of enduring scholarly value (including out-of-copyright works originally issued by other publishers) across a wide range of disciplines in the humanities and social sciences and in science and technology.

Report of the Lords of the Privy Council on Commerce and Navigation

Between His Majesty's Dominions, and the Territories belonging to the United States of America

Board of Trade

CAMBRIDGE
UNIVERSITY PRESS

CAMBRIDGE UNIVERSITY PRESS

Cambridge, New York, Melbourne, Madrid, Cape Town, Singapore,
São Paolo, Delhi, Dubai, Tokyo, Mexico City

Published in the United States of America by Cambridge University Press, New York

www.cambridge.org
Information on this title: www.cambridge.org/9781108025027

© in this compilation Cambridge University Press 2010

This edition first published 1791
This digitally printed version 2010

ISBN 978-1-108-02502-7 Paperback

A

R E P O R T

O F

The Lords of the Committee of Privy Council,
appointed for all Matters relating to
Trade and Foreign Plantations,

O N

*The Commerce and Navigation between His Majesty's
Dominions, and the Territories belonging to the
United States of America.*

28th January 1791.

At the Council Chamber, Whitehall, the 28th January 1791.

By the Right Honourable the Lords of the Committee of Council appointed for the Confideration of all Matters relating to Trade and Foreign Plantations.

———————

YOUR MAJESTY having been pleafed, by your Order in Council of the 30th September 1789, to refer to this Committee an Act paffed by the Congrefs of the United States of America on the 4th July preceding, entitled, " *An act for laying a* " *duty on goods, wares, and merchandize, imported into the United* " *States;*" and alfo, another act paffed by the faid Congrefs on the 20th of the faid month of July, entitled, " *An act impofing* " *duties on tonnage;*" and Your Majefty having directed the Committee to confider the faid acts, and report their opinion on the fame to Your Majefty; the Lords of the Committee loft no time in calling for fuch accounts, and collecting fuch other information, as

might

might beft enable them to form an opinion on the probable effects of the faid acts, and of the meafures which, in confequence thereof, it might be proper, under all the prefent circumftances, to purfue for the fecurity of the Britifh commerce and navigation. With this view, the Committee referred feveral queftions to a committee of Merchants of the City of London, concerned in the trade to the United States of America, and to the Merchants and Ship-owners of Briftol, Liverpool, and Glafgow, concerned in the fame trade : for, as this trade is principally carried on from the ports before mentioned, the Merchants and Ship-owners, refiding therein, were, in the opinion of the Committee, beft qualified to judge of the effects, which any regulation, made by the government of the faid States, is likely to produce on the Commerce, the Manufactures, and the Shipping-intereft of Your Majefty's dominions.

The Lords of the Committee thought it right alfo to apply to Your Majefty's Confuls, ftationed in the United States, for fuch information, as they, from their refidence, were beft able to afford on many parts of this fubject.

Some time of courfe elapfed before the Merchants and Ship-owners of the ports before mentioned could return anfwers to the queftions propofed to them ; and it was neceffary to allow ftill further time to Your Majefty's Confuls, refident in America, to collect and tranfmit the information required of them.

And the Committee muft confefs, that, even after they had received all the neceffary information, they found great difficulty in forming a decifive opinion on the fubject referred to them; efpecially as, in difcuffing the various points arifing out of it, they were unavoidably led to enter into a full confideration of this branch of

commerce

commerce in all its parts; and the difficulty was increaſed, when they obſerved in the anſwers of the Merchants and Ship-owners before mentioned, (who appear to have paid great attention to the queſtions propoſed to them,) that they expreſſed their ſentiments with much heſitation, and ſome difference, concerning the meaſures beſt calculated to promote their intereſts : It happened alſo, that other circumſtances afterwards occurred, which induced the Committee to think that ſome ſuſpenſion in making their Report might not be inexpedient :—But as the Duke of Leeds, one of Your Majeſty's Principal Secretaries of State, has lately acquainted this Committee, that it is Your Majeſty's intention forthwith to ſend to America a Perſon, authorized on the part of Your Majeſty, to treat with the Government of the United States on commercial as well as other matters ; and as His Grace has ſignified Your Majeſty's commands, that this Committee ſhould take into conſideration, and report, what are the propoſals, of a commercial nature, proper to be made by the Government of this country to the ſaid United States ; the Lords of the Committee have thought it their duty to reſume the Conſideration of this buſineſs, and to proceed without delay in making their Report on the whole of this extenſive ſubject.

As it may be of uſe to be informed of all, that the Merchants and Ship-owners, trading to America, have urged in ſupport of their reſpective opinions, the Lords of the Committee will place in the Appendix to this Report, the whole of the Anſwers * given by the ſaid Merchants and Ship owners to the Queſtions propoſed to them, availing themſelves in the Report, which they now preſent to Your Majeſty, of ſuch facts, ſtated in the ſaid Anſwers, as appear to the Committee to be important and well authenticated, and of ſuch arguments and calculations, as appear to be well founded, particularly

* See the Anſwers of the Merchants and Ship-owners of London, Briſtol, Liverpool, and Glaſgow, to the Queſtions referred to them, in the Appendix (A).

ſuch

fuch as have contributed in any degree to affift the Committee in forming their judgment on this occafion.

The CONNECTION which had fo long fubfifted between Great Britain and the countries now forming the United States of America, was finally diffolved by the acknowledgment of their independence in the year 1783; the ancient commercial fyftem, arifing out of that connection, of courfe ended with it; and the laws, by which the trade of thefe countries, confidered as colonies, had hitherto been regulated, ceafed to have effect :—It was neceffary therefore to adopt new principles, on which a new fyftem of commerce might be founded. But thefe States, for feveral years fubfequent to their independence, were governed in all commercial matters by feparate and diftinct Legiflatures, which were independent of each other, and had different interefts to purfue :—For fo long it was thought wife by the Government of this country to fufpend the confideration of a compleat commercial Arrangement between the faid States and Your Majefty's dominions, and to make only provifional regulations.—For this purpofe, the Britifh Legiflature, in each feffion fince the year 1783, has vefted in Your Majefty, with the advice of your Privy Council, powers fufficient for making fuch provifional regulations : but as a new Conftitution has of late been formed for the general government of the United States, to which all the Thirteen States have now acceded ; and as the fundamental articles of this Conftitution have vefted in a Prefident, in a Senate, and a Houfe of Reprefentatives, the powers requifite for regulating the commercial concern of all thefe States, which·are in this refpect now to be confidered as One Body Politic, it is certainly become neceffary to determine, by what principles the Commerce between the faid States, and the different parts of Your Majefty's dominions, fhould in future be regulated.

The Committee think it right to begin by laying before Your Majefty a fhort ftate of the meafures purfued by the Government of

this

this country, from the conclusion of the late war in 1783 to the present time, for the purpose of regulating the Commerce carried on by the subjects of the United States with Your Majesty's dominions; and, vice versâ, of the measures pursued by the Legislatures of the said States, from the year 1783 to the opening of the first session of the present Congress, for the purpose of regulating the Commerce carried on in their dominions by the subjects of Your Majesty.—The Committee will next endeavour to shew the Effects which the independence of the United States, as well as the measures before mentioned, have hitherto produced on the Commerce and Navigation of Your Majesty's dominions.

CONDUCT OF GREAT BRITAIN.

Your Majesty, by your Orders in Council, has been pleased to make the following regulations:

First—That any goods, the importation of which into this kingdom is not prohibited by law, being the growth or production of any of the territories of the United States of America, may be imported directly from thence into any of the Ports of this kingdom, not only in British ships, owned by Your Majesty's subjects, and navigated according to law, but also in ships built in the countries belonging to the United States of America, and owned by the subjects of the said States, and whereof the master and three fourths of the mariners, at least, are subjects of the United States.

OBSERVATION.

The permission, thus given for importing the before mentioned articles into Great Britain from the countries in America belonging to the United States, in any other ships than those which are built in Your Majesty's dominions, owned by Your Majesty's subjects,

and

and navigated according to law, is directly contrary to the provisions in an ancient statute of this kingdom ; which had never, till on this occasion, been dispensed with, in favour of any foreign nation, or the colony of any such nation in America: for by the 12*th Cha.* 2. *ch.* 18. *sect.* 3. " No goods or commodities whatsoever of the growth, pro-
" duction, or manufacture of any part of America, are to be im-
" ported into any of Your Majesty's European dominions in any
" other ship or vessel, than such as do truly belong to Your Ma-
" jesty's subjects, and are navigated according to law in the manner
" therein described, under the penalty of forfeiting all such goods,
" and the ship or vessel in which they are brought."—By the foregoing regulation, made in favour of the Commerce of the United States, Your Majesty has put the said Commerce, as far as relates to the ships in which any merchandize of the growth or production of the said States may be imported, upon the same footing, on which the Commerce of every independent European nation, carried on with this country, is now allowed to stand.

Secondly—Your Majesty, by the said orders in Council, has been pleased to permit, that any goods, being unmanufactured, (except fish-oil, blubber, whale-fins, and spermaceti,) and also any pig-iron, bar-iron, pitch, tar, turpentine, rosin, pot-ash, pearl-ash, indigo, masts, yards, and bowsprits, being the growth or production of any of the territories of the United States of America, may be imported directly from thence into any of the ports of this kingdom, upon payment of the same duties, as the like sorts of goods are or may be subject to, if imported from any British Island or Plantation in America ;—and that fish-oil, blubber, whale-fins, and spermaceti, and also all other goods, not herein before enumerated or described, being the growth, production, or manufacture of any of the territories of the said States, may be imported from thence into the Ports of this kingdom, upon payment of such duties of customs and excise, as are payable on the like goods upon their importation into this
kingdom

kingdom from countries not under the dominion of Your Majefty, according to the tables marked A, D, and F, annexed to the Confolidation Act; and in cafes where different duties are therein impofed upon the like goods imported from different foreign countries, then upon payment of the loweft of fuch duties.

OBSERVATION.

Your Majefty by this regulation has thought fit to grant to the Commerce of the United States, with refpect to certain articles above enumerated and defcribed (being thofe in which the Commerce of the faid States is principally carried on) the fame preference as is granted to the Commerce of the Iflands and Plantations in America, remaining under Your Majefty's dominion: And, in many of thefe articles, the Commerce of the faid States derives great benefit from the preference, thus given, to the detriment of the Commerce of other foreign nations, as will be feen by the following table:

		Duties payable if imported from the United States.			Duties payable if imported from other foreign countries.		
		l.	*s.*	*d.*	*l.*	*s.*	*d.*
Pot-afh -	per cwt.	free			0	2	3
Pearl-afh - -	per cwt.	free			0	2	3
Iron, bar -	per ton	free			2	16	2
Pitch - -	per laft	0	11	0	0	12	5
Tar - -	per laft	0	11	0	0	12	$4\frac{1}{2}$
Skins, beaver	each	0	0	1	0	0	$8\frac{1}{4}$
Tobacco -	per lb.	0	1	3	0	3	6

It is proper to add, that all woods, the produce of the countries belonging to the United States, except mafts, yards, and bowfprits, may be imported from thence duty free; whereas the like woods imported

imported from other foreign countries are fubject to various high duties, which produce a revenue of more than 250,000*l.* per annum to Great Britain.

And, with refpect to all other articles, either of produce or manufacture, not fo enumerated or defcribed in the faid Order, Your Majefty has been pleafed to put the Commerce of the United States upon the footing of the moft favoured nation, except fuch nations only, with which Your Majefty has made Treaties of Commerce, founded on the principles of reciprocity and mutual advantage.

Thirdly—Your Majefty, by the faid Orders in Council, has allowed the goods and merchandize, being the growth, production or manufacture of the territories of the United States, though imported in fhips belonging to the fubjects of the faid States, to be exempted from the Aliens-Duty.

OBSERVATION.

The goods imported in fhips belonging to all other foreign nations are fubject to the Aliens-Duty; and the Government of this country has received frequent complaints from other foreign nations of the diftinction thus made, to their prejudice ,in favour of the Commerce of the United States.

Fourthly—Your Majefty, by the faid Orders in Council, did think fit to permit to be imported into the Colonies or Iflands belonging to Your Majefty in America or the Weft Indies, in Britifh fhips only, navigated according to law, all fuch articles of the growth, production, or manufacture of any of the territories of the faid United States,
(except

(except falted provifions, and the produce of their fifheries,) as might by law before the declaration of independence have been imported from the countries belonging to the faid States into any of the faid Colonies or Iflands ; but Your Majefty, at the fame time, thought fit to prohibit any commercial intercourfe between the countries belonging to the United States of America, and the Colonies or Iflands belonging to Your Majefty in America or the Weft Indies, in fhips belonging to the fubjects of the faid United States.

OBSERVATION.

This laft regulation, firft eftablifhed by Order in Council, has fince been adopted and confirmed by act of Parliament ; and, though the people of the United States complain of this regulation more than of any other, it is not new, but is founded on the ancient law of this country, " which forbids any goods to be imported into, or " exported from, any of the Colonies belonging to Your Majefty " in Afia, Africa, or America, except in fhips belonging to Your " Majefty's fubjects, and navigated according to law :"—It is founded alfo on a principle of public law approved and adopted by all European Nations, who have ever claimed a right of reftraining the Trade and Navigation of their Colonies, in fuch manner, as in their judgment, will be moft conducive to their refpective interefts.—It might be proved, if it were neceffary, that the policy of Great Britain, in this refpect, is much more liberal than that of France or Spain.

CONDUCT

CONDUCT OF THE UNITED STATES.

The Committee will proceed, in the next place, to lay before Your Majefty a fhort Abftract of the Laws affecting the Commerce of Your Majefty's fubjects, paffed by the feveral Legiflatures of the faid States, between the year 1783, and the firft feffion of the prefent Congrefs.

The Merchants and Ship-owners, concerned in the Trade to America, have repeatedly laid before Your Majefty's Minifters an account of the Loffes, to which their Property and Commerce have been expofed by laws of this defcription.

PROHIBITIONS.

By laws, made in the provinces of New Hampfhire, Maffa-chufett's Bay, and Rhode Ifland, veffels owned, in whole or in part, by the fubjects of Great Britain, were prohibited from taking on board in thofe provinces any goods or merchandize of the growth or manufacture of thofe States, or of any other of the United States; and fuch veffels, fo loaded, were, together with their cargoes, made fubject to feizure and condemnation.—The Legiflature of Penfylvania thought fit to inveft Congrefs with a power for fifteen years to prohibit the importation or exportation of all merchandize in veffels belonging to, or navigated by, the fubjects of any Nation with whom Congrefs fhall not have formed treaties of commerce, provided Congrefs have the confent of Nine States to carry fuch Act into execution. This law, as well as all others of the fame defcrip-

tion,

tion, pointed in Terms againſt the commerce of every Nation with which Congreſs had not formed treaties of commerce, had principally, if not ſolely, in view the Commerce and Navigation of Great Britain.—By laws made in Maſſachuſett's Bay and Rhode Iſland, Congreſs was impowered to prohibit the importation of Britiſh Weſt India produce in Britiſh veſſels, whenever all the States, compoſing the Union, ſhould have veſted Congreſs with a ſimilar power.

Tonnage Duties, giving a Preference to the Ships of the United States, and of other Nations, over thoſe of Great Britain.

By a law made in Pennſylvania, a duty of 4 s. 6 d. per ton for every voyage, was impoſed on the veſſels of every nation, with which Congreſs had not made treaties of commerce.—By a law made in Maryland, a duty of 1 s. per ton was impoſed on all foreign ſhipping, except Britiſh; and a Duty of 5 s. per ton on Britiſh ſhipping.—By a law paſſed in Virginia in 1788, a duty of 6 s. per ton was impoſed on Britiſh veſſels, and 3 s. per ton on all other foreign veſſels.—By a law made in North Carolina, a duty of 5 s. per ton was impoſed on Britiſh veſſels; and a duty of 1 s. per ton on all other veſſels.

Duties on Import, giving a Preference to the Ships of the United States, and of other Nations, over thoſe of Great Britain.

By Laws paſſed in the Provinces of New Hampſhire, Maſſachuſett's Bay, and Rhode Iſland, in 1785, a duty of 6 d. currency,

being

being equal to 4¼d. sterling, was imposed on every bushel of salt, imported in ships owned, in whole, or in part, by British subjects;— and by laws passed in the Provinces of New York, and Maryland, the cargoes of British ships are, in every case, to pay double the duties imposed on those of other nations.—By a law of Virginia a tariff was established, to commence in March 1788, by which an additional duty was imposed on all merchandise imported in British ships.

Duties on Import, giving a Preference to the Pro-
duce and Manufactures of other Nations over
those of Great Britain.

By laws made in the provinces of New Hampshire, Massachusetts Bay and Rhode Island, a duty of 6 s. sterling per hundred weight is laid on cordage of British manufacture, and only half that duty, if it be of the manufacture of any other foreign nation.—By a law passed in the province of Maryland, a duty of 2 s. per cwt. was imposed on brown and clayed sugars imported from the British West India islands; and a duty of 1 s. 6 d. per cwt. on the like articles, imported from the plantations of France, Spain, Holland, Denmark, and Sweden; and a duty of 1 d. per lb. on refined sugar imported from Great Britain; and a duty of ½ d. per lb. on the like article, imported from the dominions of France, Spain, Holland, Denmark, and Sweden.—By a law passed in South Carolina in 1784, higher duties were imposed on the produce of the British West India Islands, than were payable on the like produce of the West India islands of other foreign nations;—and in Georgia similar acts were passed for the same purposes. The Committee believe that the Laws beforementioned

mentioned are by no means all that have been paſſed for the purpoſes before ſtated. The regulations made in theſe reſpects by the Legiſlatures of the ſeveral States, are ſo various, that it is hardly poſſible to obtain a complete account of them. The Merchants of Glaſgow eſtimate the tonnage duty,* impoſed in the period abovementioned, on Britiſh ſhipping through all the United States, to have been on an average 2 s. 3 d. more per ton than on American ſhips, and that this charge on a ſhip of 200 tons, amounts to 22 l. 10 s. for each voyage; and They eſtimate the duty, impoſed during the ſame period, on goods imported in Britiſh ſhips through all the United States, to be upon an average 2 per cent. more than on the like goods imported in American ſhips, and that this charge on a cargo of the value of 2000 l. amounts to 40 l.

The laws hitherto enumerated, particularly thoſe that gave a preference to the merchandiſe and ſhips of other nations over thoſe of Great Britain, were certainly unfriendly; and Your Majeſty's ſubjects have a right to complain of them : But there is another deſcription of laws paſſed, during the ſame period, by the Legiſlatures of many of theſe States, for the expreſs purpoſe of preventing or poſtponing the recovery of juſt debts, and of obliging creditors to take, as a legal tender in payment of them, depreciated paper, or other property inſtead of caſh : Such laws muſt be conſidered as deſtructive of all mercantile confidence and credit, and as contrary to every principle of honour and juſtice.

---

* The Committee have thought it right to rely in theſe reſpects very much on the calculations made by the Merchants of Glaſgow, who, from the trade they carry on, are certainly competent to judge of the accuracy of ſuch calculations. They appear alſo to have paid great attention to the queſtions referred to them.— The Merchants of this City have differed upon many points, and have made ſeparate reports; but they appear to agree nearly in their calculations.

A pre-

A pretence was taken to juftify thefe laws, by alledging that the debts, to which they relate, were contracted before the late war, and might therefore be confidered as cancelled by it.—Nothing can be more unjuft than to fuppofe that the conduct of any Sovereign (in whatever light it may be viewed) can cancel mercantile contracts, or other private and perfonal obligations, by which the fubjects of one country may have previoufly bound themfelves to the fubjects of another country, though hoftilities between the two countries may happen afterwards, from any caufe, to enfue. But even this pretence was removed by the *4th and 5th articles* of the late Definitive Treaty of Peace between Your Majefty and the United States: For by the *4th article* it was ftipulated, " That creditors on either " fide fhould meet with no lawful impediment to the recovery of " the full value in fterling money of all bonâ fide debts heretofore " contracted :" And by the *5th article* it was ftipulated, " That " Congrefs fhall earneftly recommend to the feveral States a recon- " fideration and revifion of all acts and laws regarding the premifes, " fo as to render them perfectly confiftent, not only with juftice " and equity, but with that fpirit of conciliation, which, on the " return of the bleffings of peace, fhould univerfally prevail."— The Legiflature of Great Britain has acted in full conformity to thefe juft and honourable principles: the perfons and property of American fubjects have uninterruptedly enjoyed, in every part of Your Majefty's dominions, the fame protection as the fubjects of Your Majefty; and no diftinction has ever been made in this refpect, either by the Britifh legiflature, or by Your Majefty's Courts of Juftice, to the difadvantage of the fubjects of the United States.

A particular account of the laws before defcribed, paffed by the Legiflatures of many of the States of North America, has, from time to time, been laid before Your Majefty's Minifters by fuch of Your fubjects as have feverely fuffered by thefe unjuft tranfactions :—

It

It is fufficient therefore at prefent to obferve to Your Majefty, that, in many of the States, Laws have been paffed, enacting, that in fome cafes, debts fhould be paid only by inftallments, poftponing the laft of thefe inftallments to a very diftant period ;—That in other cafes, no fuits fhould be permitted to be inftituted for a debt contracted by a citizen of the United States till a diftant period ;— That in other cafes, no execution fhould be levied till after the expiration of a certain number of years: And thefe rules have, in fome inftances, been applied, not only to debts contracted before the war, or during its continuance, but even to debts contracted fince the Peace.   Laws have alfo been paffed in fome of the States, making a depreciated paper-currency, legal tender, and even authorizing debtors to tender land at a certain valuation in fatisfaction of their debts ; and yet it has been held by the Courts of Juftice in fome of the States, that Britifh fubjects are Aliens, and, as fuch, not capable of holding lands ; fo that the land, thus affigned to a Britifh creditor in payment of his debt, by this rule of law, reverted to the State, as forfeited by the alienage of the poffeffor.—To delay the recovery of debts, it was enacted by a law in one of thefe States, that no fuit fhould be commenced, till the creditor had made application, in writing, from himfelf to his debtor for payment.—In another of thefe States, the Governor made an order, (which for a fhort time fubfifted), compelling all Britifh fubjects and factors, who had arrived there for the purpofe of collecting and recovering the debts belonging to their employers, forthwith to depart the territories of that State.

In almoft all thefe States, Laws have paffed, precluding Britifh creditors from claiming intereft, which had accrued during the continuance of the war, on any debts then owing to them.—In one of
the

the States, all demands of intereſt were declared unlawful till after the firſt of May 1786.

As late as the month of July 1787, it was laid down by the Chief Juſtice of Penſylvania in his direction to a Jury, that the laws of particular States were ſufficient to ſet aſide the uſage, which had hitherto prevailed between Britiſh and American traders, as far as related to the payment of intereſt, that had accrued during the con-tinuance of the war: And when one of the Jurors aſked him, whether the late Treaty of Peace ought not to have ſome influence on the Queſtion, the Chief Juſtice anſwered, that the Treaty of Peace only ſecured the mutual recovery of debts, when the amount was aſcertained; but that the amount of the debt was to be aſcertained by the law of the land: The Jury in this caſe accordingly deducted intereſt for ſix years and a half. Juries have in other caſes deducted eight years intereſt and a half.

It is but juſtice, however, to the late Congreſs to obſerve, that, at the ſame time that they publiſhed an account of the ratification of the late Treaty of Peace, they came to a reſolution to recommend to the ſeveral States, to conform to every part of the fifth Article before mentioned; and, by a letter written by the ſaid Congreſs in April 1787, addreſſed to the Governors of the ſeveral States, they acknow-ledged with regret, that in ſome of the States too little attention had been paid to the publick faith pledged by the late Treaty of Peace. They obſerved that, not only the obvious dictates of religion, mo-rality and national honour, but alſo the firſt principles of good policy demand a punctual compliance with engagements conſtitu-tionally made;—that the Legiſlatures of Individual States have no right to accept ſome Articles of a Treaty and reject others, or to de-cide, in what ſenſe the Citizens and Courts of Juſtice of ſuch State

ſhall

fhall underftand or interpret any particular ftipulation ;—that if any doubt fhould arife concerning the meaning of any fuch Article, the Sovereigns only, who are Parties to the Treaty, have a power, by mutual confent, to interpret and explain it;—that a contrary conduct would ferve only to introduce confufion at home, and to raife new difputes with thofe nations, with whom Treaties have been formed, which might probably terminate in open hoftilities ; They then refolved in fubftance as follows :

1ſt, That Treaties, conftitutionally made, are a part of the law of the land, and are not only independent of the will and power of particular Legiflatures, but alfo binding and obligatory upon them.

2dly, That all Acts or parts of Acts, which are now exifting in any of the States repugnant to the Treaty of Peace, ought to be forthwith repealed; as well to prevent their continuing to be executed in violation of that treaty, as to avoid the difagreeable neceffity, there might otherwife be, of raifing and difcuffing queftions touching their validity and obligation.

3dly, That it be recommended to the feveral States, to repeal all Acts repugnant to the Treaty of Peace between the United States and His Britannick Majefty, and to declare that the Courts of Law and Equity, in all cafes and queftions arifing from, or touching, the faid Treaty, fhall decide and adjudge according to the true intent and meaning of the fame.

None of the foregoing recommendations, made by the late Congrefs, were ever fully complied with, by any of the Individual States to whom they were addreffed. The Affembly of Virginia paffed an Act, which had the appearance of conforming to the laft

of

of thefe recommendations, but annexed conditions, which rendered their compliance of no effect.

The Committee will now proceed to fhew the effects, which the Independence of the United States, as well as the laws and proceedings before ftated, have hitherto produced on the Commerce and Navigation of Your Majefty's dominions.

In order to fhew the effects, fo produced on the Commerce and Navigation of Your Majefty's dominions, the Lords of the Committee will infert in this place the beft account they have been able to procure of the State of the Commerce carried on with the countries now belonging to the United States of America, and with Your Majefty's remaining Colonies in America, and with Your Majefty's Iflands in the Weft Indies; and alfo of the number and tonnage of the veffels employed therein, for fix years preceding the laft war, and for fix years fince. The trade carried on with the countries now belonging to the United States was, before the war, and is ftill fo connected with the trade carried on to the remaining Britifh Colonies in America and the Britifh Iflands in the Weft Indies, that it is impoffible to form a true judgment of the paft and prefent extent of the firft of thefe trades, and the changes that have happened in it, without taking a comprehenfive view of all thefe trades, as they are connected with, and influence each other.

The Committee will ftate; *Firft*, The Value of the Exports from Great Britain to thefe feveral countries; And *Secondly*, the Value of the Imports into Great Britain from thefe feveral countries.

Comparifon

Comparison of the Exports from Great Britain to the Countries belonging to the United States of America, before and since the War.

Value of the British Manufactures yearly exported to the countries belonging to the United States upon an average of six years before the War, ending with 1774 - - - - - 2,216,970

Ditto, of six years since the War, ending with 1789   2,119,837

Annual Decrease since the War   -   -   £ 97,133

Value of the other articles yearly exported to these States from Great Britain, upon an average of six years before the War, ending with 1774 - - 515,066

Ditto, of six years since the War, ending with 1789   213,806

Annual Decrease since the War   -   -   £ 301,260

Total Annual Decrease since the War of British Manufactures and other articles exported from Great Britain to the countries belonging to the United States   £ 398,393

Comparison of the Exports from Great Britain to the remaining British Colonies in North America, before and since the War.

Value of British Manufactures yearly exported to the remaining British Colonies in North America, on an

average

average of fix years before the War, ending with
1774   -   -   -   -   -   310,916
Ditto, on an average of fix years fince the War, ending
with 1789   -   -   -   -   603,928

Annual Increafe fince the War   -   -   £ 293,012

Value of the other articles yearly exported from Great
Britain to thefe Britifh Colonies, upon an average of
fix years before the War, ending with 1774   -   68,495
Ditto, on an average of fix years fince the War, ending
with 1789   -   -   -   -   -   225,160

Annual Increafe fince the War   -   -   £ 156,665

Total Annual Increafe, fince the War, of Britifh Ma-
nufactures and other articles exported from Great
Britain to the remaining Britifh Colonies in North
America   -   -   -   -   -   £ 449,677

*Comparifon of the Exports from Great Britain to
the Britifh Iflands in the Weft Indies, before and
fince the War.*

Value of Britifh Manufactures yearly exported to the
Britifh Iflands in the Weft Indies, on an average of
fix years before the War, ending with 1774   1,182,379
Ditto, on an average of fix years fince the War, ending
with 1789   -   -   -   -   1,297,275

Annual Increafe fince the War   -   -   £ 114,896

Value

Value of other articles yearly exported from Great
Britain to the Britifh Iflands in the Weft Indies, on an
average of fix years before the War, ending with
1774   -   -   -   -   -   167,240
Ditto, on an average of fix years fince the War, ending
with 1789   -   -   -   -   167,145

Annual Decreafe fince the War   -   -   £   95

Total Annual Increafe, fince the War, of Britifh Manufactures, and other articles, exported from Great Britain to the Britifh Iflands in the Weft Indies   -   £ 114,801

It appears from the foregoing Comparifons, that though the Value
of the Exports to the countries belonging to the United States has
annually diminifhed fince the War to the amount of 398,393 l. yet
this diminution is more than compenfated by the increafed value of
the Annual Exports, fince the War, to the remaining Britifh Colonies
in North America, and to the Britifh Iflands in the Weft Indies,
this Increafe amounting upon an average to 564,478 l. per ann. ; fo
that upon the whole, the Value of the Exports from Great Britain to
all the countries before mentioned, has increafed, upon an average
of fix years fince the War, compared with the Value thereof upon an
average of fix years before the War, in the fum of 166,085 l. :—It appears alfo, that the Increafe has been wholly in Britifh Manufactures,
and that the Decreafe has been in other articles, principally foreign
merchandize fent from Great Britain; for the Value of Britifh
Manufactures, fo exported, has annually increafed fince the War
310,775 l., and the Value of other articles, principally foreign
merchandize, has, during the fame period, annually decreafed
144,690 l.

        Comparifon

Comparifon of the Imports into Great Britain from Countries belonging to the United States of America, before and fince the War.

Value of Merchandize imported yearly into Great Britain from the countries belonging to the United States, upon an average of fix years before the War, ending with 1774   -   -   -   -   1,752,142
Ditto, on an average of fix years fince the War, ending with 1789   -   -   -   -   908,636

Annual Decreafe fince the War   -   -   £   843,506

Comparifon of the Imports into Great Britain from the remaining Britifh Colonies in North America, before and fince the War.

Value of Merchandize imported yearly into Great Britain from the remaining Britifh Colonies in North America, on an average of fix years before the War, ending with 1774   -   -   -   -   -   123,372
Ditto, on an average of fix years fince the War, ending with 1789   -   -   -   -   220,358

Annual Increafe fince the War   -   -   -   £   96,986

Comparison of the Imports into Great Britain from the British Islands in the West Indies, before and since the War.

Value of the Merchandize imported yearly from the British Islands in the West Indies, on an average of six years before the War, ending with 1774 - 3,232,119

Ditto, upon an average of six years since the War, ending with 1789 - - - - 3,903,185

Annual Increase since the War - - - £ 671,066

It appears from the three Comparisons last stated, that the Decrease in the Value of the Imports since the War, from the countries belonging to the United States of America, annually amounting to 843,506 l., has not been wholly compensated by the Increase of the Value of the Imports, during the same period, from the remaining British Colonies in North America, and from the British Islands in the West Indies, amounting together annually to 768,052 l. but that on the whole there has been a Decrease in the annual value of the Imports from all these countries, since the War, of 75,454 l. The beforementioned great Decrease in the Value of the Imports from the countries belonging to the United States of America, is nearly accounted for, by the decreased quantity of Tobacco and Rice, annually imported, since the War, into Great Britain.

The quantity of Tobacco so imported, has, upon   lbs.
an average of six years annually, decreased - 44,774,458

Being in value - £ 582,987 : 6 : 0

And

		Cwt.	qrs.	lb.
And the quantity of Rice fo imported has, in like manner, annually decreafed -		259,035	3	9

Being in value - £ 196,526 : 5 : 4

	£	s.	d.
Total Decreafe, fince the War, in the Value of Rice and Tobacco annually imported -	779,514	1	4

As long as the countries belonging to the United States were fub-ject to the Laws, that regulate the Trade of Britifh Colonies, the two commodities before mentioned could be brought from thençe only to Great Britain : They may be now carried directly to any other country that has occafion for them. Four fifths of the whole quan-rity of Tobacco and Rice, imported before the War into Great Bri-tain, were afterwards re-exported for the confumption of other countries ; and the Value of thefe commodities, fo exported, was included in the Annual Amount of the Exports from Great Britain to all countries : It was natural therefore to expect, that by the lofs of this branch of Commerce, the ftate of our Exports in general might be greatly affected. During the three years immediately fub-fequent to the War, the Value of the Annual Exports from Great Britain to all countries was not quite fo great, as it had been before the War ; but in the three years 1787, 1788, and 1789, the value of the Annual Exports from Great Britain was much greater than it had been before the War ; and the Exports in the year 1789 greatly exceeded thofe of any former year. Since 1783, there has been, from year to year, a regular Increafe of Exports from Great Bri-tain ; and the Value of the Exports of 1789 exceeds the Value of the Exports of 1784 £ 4,400,609 : 10 : 1.

It appears from the foregoing Comparifons of Exports and Im-ports, that, as the Value of the Exports to the countries now be-longing

longing to the United States has exceeded the Value of the Imports from thence fince the War in a much greater proportion than before the War, the balance of trade between Great Britain and the faid countries is now much more in favour of Great Britain than it was before the War.

It is proper in this place to take notice, that all the foregoing Comparifons relate folely to the Trade of Great Britain ; and that they do not include the Trade of Ireland with any of the countries before mentioned ; and it is right to obferve, that both the Exports and Imports of Ireland, to and from all the faid countries in America and the Weft Indies, have greatly encreafed fince the War, as well in confequence of the independence of the United States, as of the permiffion given in 1780 to the people of Ireland to carry on a direct Trade in the fame manner as the people of Great Britain with the Britifh Colonies in North America, and the Britifh Iflands in the Weft Indies.

The Committee will proceed, in the next place, to lay before Your Majefty the beft account they have been able to procure of the Number and Tonnage of the Veffels employed in the different branches of Commerce, refpectively carried on between Great Britain and the countries belonging to the United States of America, and the remaining Britifh Colonies in North America, and the Britifh Iflands in the Weft Indies.

There are many difficulties in ftating this account :—

Firft—The Account of the Number of Veffels employed in this Commerce, was not kept with the fame accuracy before the War as it is at prefent ; and the Account of their Tonnage, as kept before the War, is ftill lefs accurate. Before the paffing of the Act, *For the further encreafe and encouragement of Shipping and Navigation,*

Britifh

Britifh veffels were not furveyed with fufficient accuracy ; and the Account of their Tonnage was taken from no better authority than the declaration of the Mafter : It was then alfo for the intereft of the Mafter to diminifh the number of tons of which his veffel confifted ; as he was in confequence thereof charged with a fmaller fum for pilotage and light-houfe duties. It is fuppofed, that the amount of the tonnage of a fhip afcertained in this manner was in general one third lefs than the real tonnage.

Secondly—As before the War the countries, now under the Government of the United States, were Britifh Colonies, the veffels belonging to them, were confidered as Britifh veffels : In the Account therefore of veffels employed in thefe feveral branches of Commerce before the War, there was no diftinction made between the veffels belonging to the people of the countries now under the dominion of the United States, and fuch as belonged to the other parts of the Britifh dominions. All thefe veffels were equally confidered as Britifh fhips.

Thirdly—The Committee have not been able to procure Accounts of the Number of Veffels, and their Tonnage, employed in this trade for the fix years before the War, and the fix years fince the War, on which they have formed the averages of the Exports and Imports as before ftated : The Accounts which they have been able to procure, and on which they have formed the following averages, are of the years 1770, 1771, and 1772 before the War, and of 1787, 1788, and 1789 fince the War ; and they have chofen the three years laft mentioned, as thefe years are fubfequent to the paffing of the Act, *For the further encreafe and encouragement of Shipping and Navigation ;* from which time the Accounts of the Number of Veffels, and their Tonnage, have been kept with greater accuracy in every part of the Britifh dominions.

Veffels

Veſſels employed between Great Britain and the
countries belonging to the United States.

Number and tonnage of the veſſels clearing outwards, and employed yearly in the trade between Great Britain and the countries now belonging to the United States of America, on an
average of the years 1770, 1771, and 1772,   Ships.   Tons.
before the War   -   -   -   628——81,951

Number of ditto ſo employed, entering inwards, on
a like average   -   -   -   699——91,540

Medium of the average-number, and tonnage of
the veſſels entering inwards, and clearing outwards   -   -   -   -   663——86,745

Number and tonnage of Britiſh veſſels, and of veſſels belonging to the United States, clearing outwards, ſo employed, on an average of the years 1787, 1788, and 1789, ſince the War,	Britiſh. Ships. Tons.	American. Ships. Tons.	Total. Ships. Tons.
	272–55,785	157–25,725	429–81,510

Number and tonnage of
ditto, entering inwards,
on a like average -   251–49,405   169–27,403   420–76,808

E   Medium

(30)

Medium of the average-number, and tonnage, of British and American vessels so employed, entering inwards, and clearing outwards	British.		American.		Total.	
	Ships.	Tons.	Ships.	Tons.	Ships.	Tons.
	261	52,595	163	26,564	425	79,159

It appears from the foregoing averages, that the Number of Vessels employed in the direct Commercial Intercourse between Great Britain and the countries now belonging to the United States of America, has decreased since the War 238; and that the quantity of Tonnage has decreased since the War 7,586 tons. The decrease of the tonnage appears to be much less than the decrease of the number of the ships, and the decrease of the tonnage inwards is much greater than that of the tonnage outwards. The reason that the quantity of the Tonnage in general appears to be less decreased than the Number of Ships is:

First, That larger ships are now employed in this, as well as in every other branch of Commerce, than formerly.

Secondly, The imperfect manner of taking the account of the Tonnage before the War, as before stated, which was then estimated, for the reasons before mentioned, about one third less than it really was.

The greater decrease of the tonnage inwards, compared with that of the tonnage outwards, is to be imputed to the diminished importation of the bulky articles of Rice and Tobacco, as before stated.

It

It appears, by the foregoing account of the veffels employed in this trade fince the War, that the Number of Britifh veffels, fo employed, exceeds the Number of American veffels, fo employed, 98 fhips ; and the Quantity of Britifh Tonnage, fo employed, exceeds the Quantity of American Tonnage, fo employed, 26,031 tons.

As there was no diftinction before the war between fhips belonging to the inhabitants of the countries now under the dominion of the United States, and the other parts of the Britifh Dominions, it is impoffible to ftate, with certainty, what was the proportion of each defcription of fhips then employed in this branch of Commerce.

The Veffels, fo employed, were then of three forts.

Firft—Veffels belonging to Merchants refident in the Britifh European Dominions.

Secondly—Veffels belonging to Britifh Merchants, occafionally refident in thofe Colonies, that now form the United States.

Thirdly—Veffels belonging to Merchants, who were Natives and permanent Inhabitants of thofe Colonies, that now form the United States.

The following Table will fhew the Proportion of each Defcription of Veffels, claffed in the manner before mentioned, then employed in this Branch of Commerce, according to the beft information that can be obtained :

New

	Proportion of veſſels belonging to Merchants reſident in the Britiſh European dominions.	Proportion of veſſels belonging to Britiſh Merchants occaſionally reſident in thoſe Colonies that now form the United States.	Proportion of veſſels belonging to Merchants, who were Natives and permanent Inhabitants of thoſe Colonies that now form the United States.
New England	1-8th	1-8th	6-8ths
New York	3-8ths	3-8ths	2-8ths
Penſylvania	2-8ths	3-8ths	3-8ths
Maryland and Virginia	6-8ths	1-8th	1-8th
North Carolina	5-8ths	2-8ths	1-8th
S. Carolina and Georgia	5-8ths	2-8ths	1-8th

From the foregoing Table it is evident, that the Proportion of Veſſels, claſſed under the beforementioned deſcriptions, varied according to the different Colonies, now forming the United States, with which the Commerce of Great-Britain was then carried on; the quantity of ſhipping ſo employed which belonged, either to the inhabitants of Great Britain, or to Britiſh Merchants occaſionally reſident in the ſaid Colonies, being much greater in the commercial intercourſe, then carried on with the Southern Colonies, than with the Northern Colonies, particularly thoſe of New England.—But, upon the whole, there is reaſon to believe, from calculations founded on the foregoing Table, as well as from other information, that the Proportion of Tonnage, employed before the War in this branch of Commerce, which belonged to the Inhabitants of Great Britain, was about 4-8ths and an half; and the Proportion, which belonged to Britiſh Merchants, occaſionally reſident in the Colonies now forming the United States, was about one-eighth and an half, making together nearly ſix-eighths of the whole; and that the Proportion of Tonnage

nage fo employed, which belonged to Merchants, who were then Natives and permanent Inhabitants of the Colonies now forming the United States, was rather more than two-eighths of the whole. At prefent the Proportion of Tonnage, employed in this branch of Commerce, belonging to the Merchants of Great Britain, is nearly fix-eighths of the whole; and the Proportion of Tonnage, belonging to the Merchants of the United States, is rather more than two-eighths of the whole; fo that, in this view of the fubject, though the Quantity of Shipping, employed between Great Britain and the countries now under the dominion of the United States, has fince the War decreafed on the whole in the degree before ftated, yet, allowing for this decreafe, the fhare of the fhipping which belongs to the Merchants of Great Britain, has encreafed in the proportion of one-eighth and an half; (the fhare of the fhipping, which before the War belonged to Britifh Merchants, occafionally refident in the Colonies now forming the United States, being transferred to Merchants refident in Great Britain), and the fhare of the fhipping fo employed, which now belongs to Merchants, fubjects of the United States, and permanent Inhabitants thereof, is nearly the fame as it was before the War.

Veffels employed between Great Britain and the remaining Britifh Colonies in North America.

	Ships.	Tons.
Number and Tonnage of Britifh veffels clearing outwards, and employed yearly in the trade between Great Britain and the remaining Britifh Colonies in North America, on an average of the Years 1770, 1771, and 1772, before the War	250	9,582

Number

	Ships.	Tons.

Number and Tonnage of ditto, fo employed, entering inwards, on a like average 273–12,857

Medium of the Average-Number and Tonnage of Britifh veffels entering inwards, and clearing outwards 261–11,219

Number and Tonnage of Britifh veffels, clearing outwards, employed in this trade, on an average of the years 1787, 1788, and 1789, fince the War 486–61,858

Number and Tonnage of ditto fo employed, entering inwards, on a like average - - 249–30,355

Medium of the Average-Number and Tonnage of Britifh Veffels entering inwards, and clearing outwards - - - 367–46,106

By the foregoing Averages it appears, that the Number of Veffels employed between Great Britain and the remaining Colonies in North America, being all Britifh fhips, has increafed fince the War in the proportion of about One-half, being 106 veffels more than it was before the War; and the Quantity of Tonnage has increafed 34,887 tons, being in the proportion of about four times more than it was before the War.

Veffels employed between Great Britain and the Britifh Iflands in the Weft Indies.

Number and Tonnage of Britifh veffels clearing outwards, and employed yearly in the trade between Great Britain and the Britifh Iflands in the Weft
Indies,

	Ships.	Tons.
Indies, on an average of the years 1770, 1771, and 1772, before the War - - -	420	75,143

Number and Tonnage of ditto, fo employed, entering inwards, on a like average   - -   563–85,821

Medium of the Average-Number and Tonnage of Britifh veffels, entering inwards, and clearing outwards   - - - -   491–80,482

Number and Tonnage of Britifh veffels clearing outwards, and employed yearly in the trade between Great Britain and the Britifh Iflands in the Weft Indies, on an average of the years 1787, 1788, and 1789, fince the War   - -   531–128,207

Number and Tonnage of ditto, fo employed, entering inwards, on a like average   - -   588–139,265

Medium of the Average-Number and Tonnage of Britifh veffels, entering inwards, and clearing outwards   - - - -   559–133,736

By thefe laft averages it appears, that the Number of Veffels employed between Great Britain and the Britifh iflands in the Weft Indies, being all Britifh fhips, is, fince the War, 68 fhips more than before the War, and has therefore increafed in the proportion of about one-feventh; and that the Quantity of Tonnage is, fince the War, 53,254 tons more than it was before the War, and has therefore increafed in the proportion of more that five-eighths. It is of importance alfo to obferve, that, before the War, a part of the fhips annually employed in bringing to Great Britain

the

the produce of the Weſt India Iſlands, was built in the countries now belonging to the United States of America. Theſe ſhips were in general loaded in the Northern States with lumber and proviſions, and conſigned to Merchants in the Weſt Indies, where their cargoes were ſold, and being then freighted with Sugar, and other Weſt India produce, they proceeded to Great Britain, where they were ſold at a rate conſiderably under the price, for which veſſels of the ſame di-menſions could be built in Great Britain. Their number is ſuppoſed to have been about fifty annually; and it is for this reaſon, that the number of ſhips, entering inwards before the War, appears by the fore-going accounts, to have exceeded the number of ſhips clearing out-wards, in a much greater proportion than it does at preſent. Since the War, the ſhips employed in this branch of Commerce are principally built in Great Britain ; and as theſe ſhips, and the ſailors with which they are manned, have a more immediate Connection with the Mo-ther Country, it is certain that they contribute in a much greater degree, than the ſhips which they have replaced, to increaſe the efficient Strength of Great Britain as a Naval Power.

Veſſels employed between the remaining Britiſh Co-lonies in North America, and the Countries be-longing to the United States.

Number and Tonnage of Britiſh veſſels clearing out-
    wards, and employed yearly in the trade between
    the remaining Britiſh Colonies in North America,
    and the countries which were then Britiſh Colonies,
    but now form the United States of America, on an

	Ships.	Tons.
average of the years 1770, 1771, and 1772, be-fore the War - - - -	250—	9,582

Number

	Ships.	Tons.
Number and Tonnage of ditto, fo employed, entering inwards, on a like average - -	276	12,857

Medium of the Average-Number and Tonnage of Britifh veffels entering inwards and clearing outwards - - - - - 263—11,219

Number and Tonnage of Britifh veffels clearing outwards, and employed yearly in the Trade between the remaining Britifh Colonies in North America, and the countries belonging to the United States, on an average of the years 1787, 1788, and 1789, fince the War - - - - 208—15,135

Number and Tonnage of ditto, fo employed, entering inwards, on a like average - - 269—15,524

Medium of the Average-Number and Tonnage of Britifh veffels entering inwards and clearing outwards - - - - - 238—15,329

The Number of the veffels, fo ftated, includes their repeated Voyages ; and it appears that the Number has decreafed, fince the War, 25 veffels, or about one-tenth : But the quantity of the Tonnage has increafed 4,110 tons, or about one-third. The veffels, employed before the War in this branch of Trade, might lawfully belong to the Inhabitants of the countries now under the Dominion of the United States ; it is certain they then owned much the greateft fhare of thefe veffels : But veffels fo employed can now belong only to the Inhabitants of the remaining Colonies, or of fome other part of the

F

Britifh

Britiſh Dominions: A great part of this Branch of Freight may be
conſidered therefore as a new acquiſition, and was obtained by the
wiſe policy, which Your Majeſty thought proper to adopt by Your
Order in Council of 18th June 1784.

*Veſſels employed between the Britiſh Iſlands in the
Weſt Indies, and the Countries belonging to the
United States.*

	Ships.	Tons.
Number and Tonnage of Britiſh veſſels clearing outwards, and employed yearly in the Trade between the Britiſh Iſlands in the Weſt Indies, and the Countries belonging to the United States, on an average of the years 1770, 1771, and 1772, before the War - -	2,172—	103,540
Number and Tonnage of ditto, ſo employed, entering inwards, on a like average - -	2,297—	111,939
Medium of the Average-Number and Tonnage of Britiſh veſſels, entering inwards, and clearing outwards - - - -	2,234—	107,739
Number and Tonnage of Britiſh veſſels clearing outwards, and employed yearly in the Trade between the Britiſh Iſlands in the Weſt Indies, and the Countries belonging to the United States, on an average of the years 1787, 1788, and 1789, ſince the War - -	510—	57,904

Number

	Proportion of vessels belonging to Merchants resident in the British European dominions.	Proportion of vessels belonging to British Merchants occasionally resident in those Colonies that now form the United States.	Proportion of vessels belonging to Merchants, who were Natives and permanent Inhabitants of those Colonies that now form the United States.
New England	1-8th	1-8th	6-8ths
New York	3-8ths	3-8ths	2-8ths
Penſylvania	2-8ths	3-8ths	3-8ths
Maryland and Virginia	6-8ths	1-8th	1-8th
North Carolina	5-8ths	2-8ths	1-8th
S. Carolina and Georgia	5-8ths	2-8ths	1-8th

From the foregoing Table it is evident, that the Proportion of Veſ-sels, claſſed under the beforementioned deſcriptions, varied according to the different Colonies, now forming the United States, with which the Commerce of Great-Britain was then carried on; the quantity of ſhipping ſo employed which belonged, either to the inhabitants of Great Britain, or to Britiſh Merchants occaſionally reſident in the ſaid Colonies, being much greater in the commercial intercourſe, then carried on with the Southern Colonies, than with the Northern Colonies, particularly thoſe of New England.—But, upon the whole, there is reaſon to believe, from calculations founded on the fore-going Table, as well as from other information, that the Proportion of Tonnage, employed before the War in this branch of Commerce, which belonged to the Inhabitants of Great Britain, was about 4-8ths and an half; and the Proportion, which belonged to Britiſh Merchants, occaſionally reſident in the Colonies now forming the United States, was about one-eighth and an half, making together nearly ſix-eighths of the whole; and that the Proportion of Ton-

nage

has operated to the Increafe of Britifh Navigation, compared to that of the United States, in a double Ratio; but it has taken from the Navigation of the United States more than it has added to that of Great Britain.

Veffels employed between the remaining Britifh Colonies in North America, and the Britifh Iflands in the Weft Indies.

	Ships.	Tons.
Number and Tonnage of Britifh veffels clearing outwards, and employed yearly in the Trade between the remaining Britifh Colonies in North America and the Britifh Iflands in the Weft Indies, on an average of the years 1770, 1771, and 1772, before the War - - -	15—	753
Number and Tonnage of ditto, fo employed, entering inwards, on a like average - -	23—	1,240
Medium of the Average-Number and Tonnage of Britifh veffels, entering inwards, and clearing outwards - - - -	19—	996
Number and Tonnage of Britifh veffels, clearing outwards, and employed yearly in the Trade between the remaining Britifh Colonies in North America and the Britifh Iflands in the Weft Indies, on an average of the years 1787, 1788, and 1789, fince the War - - -	142—	12,696

Number

	Ships,	Tons.

Number and Tonnage of ditto, fo employed, entering
   inwards, on a like average - - 171—16,331

Medium of the Average-Number and Tonnage of
   Britifh Veffels, entering inwards, and clearing outwards - - - - 156—14,513

The Account of the Number of Veffels, from whence thefe Averages are taken, includes their repeated Voyages. The Number of Veffels fo employed has encreafed fince the War 137 Ships, being feven times more than it was before the War: And the quantity of Tonnage has encreafed 13,517 Tons, being thirteen times more than it was before the War. Many cf thefe Veffels before the War belonged to the Inhabitants of the Countries, which were then Britifh Colonies, but are now under the Dominion of the United States: They can now only belong to Britifh Subjects, refident in fome part of your Majefty's prefent Dominions: A part of thefe Veffels therefore may be confidered as a new acquifition in confequence of the Order in Council before mentioned.

The great Encreafe of thefe Veffels is to be imputed to the improvement of thefe remaining Colonies, in confequence of the great number of Refugees, who have reforted thither: It is to be imputed alfo to the more frequent Intercourfe, that fubfifts at prefent between thefe Colonies and the Britifh Iflands in the Weft Indies, and to the great number of fhips belonging to thefe Colonies, or to fome other part of Your Majefty's prefent Dominions, which go from Newfoundland to the Britifh Iflands in the Weft Indies with fifh, a branch of Freight, which was almoft wholly engroffed before the War, by Merchants, who were permanent inhabitants of the

countries

countries then Britifh Colonies, but which are now under the dominion of the United States, and from which Branch of Freight
the fubjects of thefe States are at prefent entirely excluded.

As the Refult of the foregoing Deduction, the Committee have
thought fit to caufe the following Table to be prepared; Allowance is
therein made for the repeated Voyages, which the Veffels, employed
in thefe different Branches of Trade, are fuppofed to make in each
year; and the Number and Tonnage of the Veffels is reduced in due
proportion. This Table will fhew Your Majefty, at one view, the
Encreafe and Decreafe of Veffels and Tonnage employed in thefe
various branches of Navigation, and how far the Balance on the
whole is at prefent in favour of Great Britain.

1ft.

Veffels, and their Tonnage, employed between Great Britain and the United States —

2d.

Veffels, and their Tonnage, employed between Great Britain and the remaining British Colonies in North America — — — — — — — }

3d.

Veffels, and their Tonnage, employed between Great Britain and the British Iflands in the Weft Indies —

4th.

(a) Veffels, and their Tonnage, employed between the remaining British Colonies and the United States —

5th.

(b) Veffels, and their Tonnage, employed between the British Iflands in the Weft Indies and the United States

6th.

(c) Veffels, and their Tonnage, employed between the remaining British Colonies and the British Iflands in the Weft Indies — — — — — — }

RECAPITULATION, containing the Increafe and Decreafe un and the Increafe and

	British.	
	Veffels.	Tons.
Increafe on the 2d Branch of Freight —	139	36,289
Ditto on the 3d ditto — —	99	58,285
Ditto on the 4th ditto — —	115	8,350
Ditto on the 5th ditto — —	88	16,423
Ditto on the 6th ditto — —	51	4,754
Total Increafe —	492	124,101
Decreafe on the 1ft Branch of Freight — —	236	12,463
Balance of Increafe —	256	111,638

(a) The Number of Veffels, and their Tonnage, employed in this Branch of Freight, was divided
(b) The Number of Veffels in this Branch of Freight was divided by 3, as it is eftimated that thef
(c) The Number of Veffels, and their Tonnage, employed in this Branch of Freight, was divided

Before the War.				Since the War.			
Veffels, and their Tonnage, belonging to Merchants refident in the prefent Britifh dominions, or to Britifh Merchants occafionally refident in the countries which were then Britifh Colonies, but now form the United States.		Veffels belonging to Merchants who were Natives and permanent Inhabitants of the countries which were then Britifh Colonies, but now form the United States.		Veffels belonging to Subjects of the prefent Britifh dominions.		Veffels belonging to Subjects of the United States.	
Veffels.	Tons.	Veffels.	Tons.	Veffels.	Tons.	Veffels.	Tons.
497	65,058	165	21,686	261	52,595	163	26,564
228	9,816	32	1,402	367	46,106	—	—
460	75,451	30	5,030	559	133,736	—	—
43	1,869	131	5,609	158	10,219	—	—
93	4,489	651	31,423	181	20,912	—	—
1	83	4	249	52	4,837	—	—
1,322	156,766	1,013	65,399	1,578	268,405	163	26,564

der the before mentioned different Branches of Freight, Decreafe on the Whole.

	American.	
	Veffels.	Tons.
Decreafe on the 1ft	2	—
Ditto on the 2d	32	1,402
Ditto on the 3d	30	5,030
Ditto on the 4th	131	5,609
Ditto on the 5th	651	31,423
Ditto on the 6th	4	249
Total Decreafe	850	43,713
Increafe on the 1ft	—	4,877
Balance of Decreafe	850	38,836

by 1½, as it is eftimated that thefe Veffels make 1½ voyage in a year.
e Veffels make three voyages in a year.
by 3, as it is eftimated that thefe Veffels make three voyages in a year.

The Committee think it will throw further light on this Subject, if they lay before Your Majefty an Account of the Veffels that were built in the Ports of the countries now forming the United States in the year 1772, compared with the Number of Veffels that were building in the Ports of the faid States in the year 1789. This Comparifon will prove to Your Majefty, how greatly the Trade of Ship-building has declined in thefe countries fince they were no longer a Part of Your Majefty's Dominions, and confequently how very much the Number of Ships, belonging to them, muft have decreafed.

An Account of the Number of Ships and Brigs built in the Ports of the United States in the year 1772, compared with the like Veffels building in the faid States in 1789*.

States.	1772.		1789.	
	Veffels.	Tons.	Veffels.	Tons.
New Hampfhire - - - -	—	—	6	—
Maffachufets - - - -	—	—	5	—
Rhode Ifland - - - -	—	—	—	—
Connecticut - - - - -	—	—	—	—
Total of the New England Provinces	123	18,149	11	0
New York - - - -	15	1,640	—	—
New Jerfey - - - -	1	80	1	200
Penfylvania - - - - -	18	2,897	14	2,966
Maryland - - - - -	8	1,626	5	1,200
Virginia - - - - -	7	933	—	—
North Carolina - - - -	3	253	—	—
South Carolina - - - -	2	213	—	—
Georgia - - - - -	5	753	—	—
TOTAL	182		31	

* In the Account of Ships and Brigs built in the Ports of the United States in the year 1772, which has been laid before the Committee, there is no Specification of the Numbers built in each of the New England Provinces, but a Total only of the Number and Tonnage of Veffels built in all thefe Provinces : and Mr. Bond, Conful at Philadelphia, who fent the Account of the Veffels building in 1789, has not given the Tonnage of the Eleven Veffels then building in the provinces of New Hampfhire and Maffachufets' Bay : So that it is not poffible to make a Comparifon of the Quantity of Tonnage of which the Veffels in the foregoing Table confifts.

The

The Committee have received from Mr. Bond, Your Majefty's Conful at Philadelphia, very accurate Accounts of the Number of Veffels and Quantity of Tonnage, employed in the Trade to and from the Port of Philadelphia, where he refides, in the years 1773, 1774, and 1775, diftinguifhing the Veffels and Tonnage belonging to the Inhabitants of Great Britain—thofe belonging to the Inhabitants of Philadelphia—and thofe belonging to the Inhabitants of the United States, including Philadelphia; and alfo, a like Account of the Number of Veffels and Quantity of Tonnage fo employed in the years 1788 and 1789, diftinguifhing the Veffels and Tonnage belonging to the Inhabitants of the prefent Britifh dominions,—and thofe belonging to the fubjects of the United States.—As thefe Accounts throw further light on this important fubject, the Committee will infert them in the Appendix *.

It appears by the firft of thefe Accounts, that the Tonnage of the Veffels belonging to the Inhabitants of Great Britain, clearing out from the Port of Philadelphia in the years 1773, 1774, and 1775, was not equal to one fourth part of the Tonnage of the Veffels fo clearing out, and belonging only to the Inhabitants of Philadelphia; and that it was equal only to two elevenths of the Tonnage of the Veffels belonging to the Inhabitants of the Countries now forming the United States, including Philadelphia.

It appears by the fecond of thefe Accounts, that the Tonnage of the Veffels belonging to the Inhabitants of the prefent Britifh dominions, clearing out from the Port of Philadelphia in the years 1788 and 1789, amounted to within One Fifth of the Tonnage of all the Veffels belonging to the Inhabitants of the United States, including Philadelphia, which cleared out from the fame Port in the fame years:—And Mr. Bond alledges,

* See thefe Accounts in the Appendix, (B).

that

that the Tonnage of the Veſſels belonging to the Inhabitants of the preſent Britiſh dominions, now employed in the Port of Philadelphia, in
that branch of trade which is called the Over-ſea Trade, is full four
fifths of the Tonnage of all the Veſſels ſo employed.

To compleat the foregoing Accounts, the Committee thought it right
to enquire, what Share the Ships of other European nations, beſides
Great Britain, have obtained in the Commerce carried on with the
United States of America.—It is well known, that the expectation,
which theſe nations entertained of acquiring a conſiderable ſhare in this
branch of trade, in caſe the Britiſh Colonies, which now form the
United States, could eſtabliſh their independence, operated as a
ſtrong motive to induce many of them to be adverſe to the Cauſe of
Great Britain during the late War; and inclined ſome of them, by
degrees, to take a part in the Conteſt.

The following Account is the beſt, that the Committee have been
able to procure of the Veſſels belonging to other European nations,
beſides Great Britain, which entered the principal Ports of the
United States in the following years:

N E W - Y O R K.

1789.	Ships.	Brigantines.	Schooners.	Sloops.	Suppoſed Tonnage, according to the American admeaſurement.
Portugueſe	3	4	1	0	1,380
Spaniſh	3	3	1	4	1,580
Dutch	2	1	0	0	960
French	1	5	0	0	1,000
Swedes	0	2	0	0	400
Total	9	15	2	4	5,320

G

PHILADELPHIA.

1788.	Ships.	Brigan-tines.	Schoon-ers.	Sloops.	Suppofed Tonnage, according to the American admeafurement.
French - -	1	4	1	0	692
Dutch - - -	0	4	4	2	1,022
Spanifh - -	7	6	4	0	2,335
Portuguefe - -	0	3	0	0	321
Swedifh - -	0	2	0	1	430
Danifh - -	0	1	0	0	157
Pruffian - - -	0	2	0	0	388
Total -	8	22	9	3	5,345

CHARLES-TOWN.

1787.	Ships.	Brigan-tines.	Schoon-ers.	Sloops.	Tonnage
Spain - - -	0	2	39	3	1,073
France - -	0	4	2	2	715
United Netherlands -	1	4	0	0	799
Altona - -	1	0	0	0	280
Bremen - - -	0	1	0	0	193
Denmark - -	0	1	0	0	164
Hamburgh - -	0	1	0	0	130
Auftria - - -	0	1	0	0	127
Total -	2	14	41	5	3,481

The foregoing Tables will fhew, in what proportion the feveral European Nations, therein mentioned, have acquired a fhare in the
Commerce

Commerce carried on in three of the principal Ports of the United States. The Committee have not been able to procure like accounts of the fhips belonging to thofe European Nations, which have been employed in the trade carried on in the other ports of the United States ; but, from information laid before them, they have reafon to think, that the Tonnage of the Veffels belonging to European Nations, befides Great Britain, which traded to the ports of Virginia in the year 1789, amounted to 2,664 tons;—That the Tonnage of the Veffels of the like defcription, which traded to the ports of Maryland in the year 1789, amounted to 2,348 tons ;—That the Tonnage of the Veffels of the like defcription, which traded to the ports of North Carolina in the year 1789, amounted to about 3,000 tons ;—That the Tonnage of the Veffels of the like defcription, which traded to the ports of Georgia in the year 1789, amounted to about 2,500 tons ;—That the Tonnage of the Veffels of the like defcription, which traded to the Ports of Maffachufet's Bay in the year 1789, amounted to 1,758 tons.

The Committee have no information of the Veffels of the like defcription, which have been employed in the Commerce carried on with the other United States ; but if we add to the foregoing quantity of tonnage, amounting to 26,416 tons, one-fourth more for all the remaining ports of the United States of America, the whole of the Tonnage of Veffels of the defcription before mentioned, employed in the Commerce with the United States, will in fuch cafe amount to 33,020 tons, which is but little more than one-fourth of the Tonnage of the Veffels belonging to Britifh Merchants in all the different Branches of this Commerce, not making Allowance in either cafe for repeated Voyages.

Imme-

Immediately after the Peace, the Merchants of Foreign Nations entered with great zeal into the Trade which was then for the firſt time laid open to them, with the Countries belonging to the United States of America ; but theſe Merchants ſoon found that the great expeƈtations they had entertained were not likely to be realized.—They learned by experience that this Trade was not to be carried on, without truſting the Americans with their goods, and without giving them longer credit than is uſually given in the Trade carried on to European Countries : Many of them ſent their veſſels with ſupercargoes on board, who would not ſell the goods, with which they were entruſted, but for ready money, or in barter for an immediate return in the produce of the country : Several of theſe ſupercargoes met with an ill reception. To theſe circumſtances it is owing, that the Merchants beforementioned are now leſs diſpoſed to engage in this Branch of Commerce, and that many Britiſh veſſels are now aƈtually employed in carrying the Produce of America direƈtly to the markets of other European Nations.

The Lords of the Committee have thought it right to puſh their enquiries, on all that relates to the Commerce carried on with the United States, and to the Shipping employed therein, to the utmoſt extent ; as it appeared to them to be of the greateſt importance to aſcertain, with as much accuracy as poſſible, the Effeƈts which the late Revolution in North America has hitherto produced on the Commerce and Navigation of Your Majeſty's preſent dominions.—To enable the Committee to form a true judgment of what may be the probable Effeƈts of the two Aƈts referred by Your Majeſty to their conſideration, or of any other meaſures which the preſent Congreſs may purſue, and to ſuggeſt, in conſequence thereof, what Syſtem of Policy it may be adviſeable for Your Majeſty's government to adopt,

in

in order to counteract the evil effects of such measures, it was absolutely necessary to be informed, how far the Acts, and other Proceedings of the late Congress, or of the Legislatures of the separate States, have hitherto operated to the disadvantage of British Commerce and Navigation. It is true that the Merchants and Ship-owners of London, Bristol, Liverpool and Glasgow, in the Reports before mentioned, all agree in asserting, that the Commerce and Shipping-interest of Great-Britain have, in the direct intercourse between Great Britain and the United States, suffered in a certain degree, by the distinctions made to their disadvantage, in favour of the Commerce and Shipping of the United States, and of other foreign nations.—These distinctions may perhaps have contributed to diminish the advantages, which might otherwise have been derived from this trade: But it is evident, from the foregoing comprehensive view of the various Branches of Commerce and Navigation, to which these accounts refer, that the Exports from Great Britain to all the countries before mentioned, (which is the most valuable part of this Commerce,) have increased since the War, on an average, £ 166,085 per annum; and that the Imports into Great Britain from the said countries have decreased since the War, on an average, only £ 75,454 per annum; and that the Number of Ships belonging to the Merchants resident in the present British dominions, employed in all these different Branches of Commerce, has increased since the War, on an average, annually 256; and that the Quantity of their Tonnage has increased 111,638 Tons; and in like manner, that the Number of Ships, belonging to the subjects of the United States, so employed, has decreased 850 Ships, and the Quantity of their Tonnage has decreased 38,836 Tons.—If indeed we suppose that the Tonnage of the Vessels, employed in these Branches of Commerce, was estimated

before

before the War at one-third lefs than it really was, as before ftated, the Increafe of the Tonnage of the Veffels, belonging to Merchants refident in the prefent Britifh dominions, will in fuch cafe be only 59,384 Tons ; and the Decreafe of the Tonnage of Veffels belonging to Merchants, that are fubjects of the United States, will in fuch cafe amount to 60,634 Tons.—It is proper to add, that the inhabitants of the countries, which now form the United States, had before the War fome fhare in the circuitous Commerce of Great Britain, by trading from one foreign Port to another, and returning occafionally to a Britifh Port : They have fince the War loft the Benefit arifing from the Freight employed in that circuitous Trade, whatever the amount of it may have been; and the whole of it now belongs to the Inhabitants of the prefent Britifh dominions :—It appears alfo, from what has been before ftated, that the Inhabitants of the Countries now belonging to the United States, built in the year 1772, 182 top-fail veffels; and that, in the year 1789, the number of fuch veffels, building in the Ports of the United States, was only 31 :—It appears laftly, that the Tonnage of the Veffels, which belong to the fubjects of all the nations of Europe, befides Great Britain, now employed in the Trade with the United States, in the whole amounts to but little more than one-fourth of the Tonnage of the Ships, fo employed, belonging to the fubjects of the prefent Britifh dominions *.

The

---

* Subfequent to the Time when this Report was compleated, and prefented to His Majefty, the Government of the United States have publifhed a Paper, which contains an Account of the Tonnage of the Veffels entering the feveral Ports of the United States, from the 1ft October 1789, to the 30th September 1790. The Account is as follows :

An

The Lords of the Committee will proceed, in the next place, to give an Account of the new Form of Government lately eftablifhed in the United

---

An Account of the Tonnage of Veffels entered into the United States of America, from the 1ſt October 1789, to the 30th September 1790, diſtinguiſhing each State according to the Magnitude of it's Tonnage; and diſtinguiſhing the American from Foreign Veſſels.

States.	American.				European.			Recapitulation.
	Coaſting Veſſels.	Fiſhing Veſſels.	Veſſels in the Over-ſea Trade.	Total Tonnage.	Veſſels belonging to Great Britain, including Ireland.	Veſſels belonging to other Nations.	Total Tonnage of the whole.	
Maſſachuſets -	53,073	24,826	99,124	177,023	19,493	853	197,369	Total Tonnage of each Country, viz. Tons.
Pennſylvania -	6,055	—	51,594	57,649	42,605	9,665	109,919	United States - - 503,177
Virginia - -	9,914	55	33,560	43,529	56,273	4,092	103,894	Great Britain 222,347
New York. -	6,203	—	42,072	48,275	36,918	6,921	92,114	Ireland - 3,147½
Maryland -	16,099	60	39,272	55,431	23,339	9,485	88,255	————— 225,494½
* South Carolina	508	—	16,871	17,379	18,725	4,256	40,360	France - 13,435½
† North Carolina	5,723	—	24,219	29,942	4,941	244	35,127	Holland - 8,815½
Connecticut -	6,330	—	24,286	30,616	2,556	—	33,172	Spain - - 8.551¼
Georgia - -	1,090	—	9,544	10,634	15,041	1,570	27,245	Portugal - 2,924
New Hampſhire	1,670	473	11,376	13,519	3,458	34	17,011	Denmark - 1,619¾
‡ Rhode Iſland	1,626	838	7,061	9,525	95	221	9,841	Germany - 1,368
Delaware - -	1,061	—	3,080	4,141	1,783	—	5,924	Pruſſia - - 394
New Jerſey -	3,429	—	2,085	5,514	267	79	5,860	Sweden - - 311½
								————— 37,419½
Total	112,781	26,252	364,144	503,177	225,494	37,420	766,091	Total - - 766,091

* In the Returns from Charles Town, one Quarter is wanting, and not included.
† The Returns from this State did not commence till 11th March 1790.
‡ The Returns from this State did not commence till 21ſt June 1790.

Note.—This Table contains an Account of the Tonnage of Veſſels entering the ſeveral Ports of the United States, in a period ſubſequent to any of thoſe years, on which the Averages ſtated in the Report, were formed. It contains an Account of all the Tonnage belonging to the Subjects of the United States of America, employed in every Part of their Foreign Trade, their Coaſting Trade, and their Fiſheries, which entered their Ports during that Period, but does not diſtinguiſh what Part of it was employed in their Foreign Trade with the Britiſh Dominions. On the other hand, the Account

given

United States, as far as it relates to the Commerce of the said States, and of the Principles on which it is formed; and of such of the measures

---

given in the Report, is only of so much of the Tonnage of the United States, as was employed during those years in the various Branches of Commerce with such Parts of the British Dominions, with which they are allowed now to trade, in Ships belonging to the said States. This Table contains also, an Account of the Tonnage of British Vessels employed during that Period, in the Trade with the United States, and makes the Quantity thereof apparently much greater than that stated in the Report, as employed therein, during the preceding years, on which the Averages were formed.— But it should be observed, that in the period to which the Table refers, many Events happened, which would necessarily increase the Quantity of Tonnage employed in the various Branches of Commerce carried on with the United States. The great Demand for Corn in almost every Country of Europe, during the latter part of the year 1789, and till the harvest of 1790, was the Cause that many more Ships were freighted during that period, for the purpose of bringing Corn from America, than ever had been before. It is well known, that many Ships sailed from Great Britain upon Speculation for this Purpose only; and that the Demand for Corn in Europe more than doubled the usual Price of Wheat in America; and that the Price of Freight from America was considerably raised on that Account.—For these Reasons, the Quantity of American Tonnage as well as the Quantity of Foreign Tonnage, and particularly British, that entered the Ports of New York, Pensylvania, Virginia, and Maryland, (which are the principal Corn Countries of the United States,) was much greater in this Period than in the years to which the Report refers.—It happened also, that in this year, the Revolution in France induced the several French Colonies in the West Indies to open their Ports for American Ships in a much greater degree than they were opened before. This Circumstance must necessarily have increased the American Shipping employed in the Intercourse between the Countries belonging to the United States and the French Islands in the West Indies. —— It is proper also to observe, that the Quantity of American as well as of British and other Foreign Tonnage, as stated in this Table, appears to be greater than it actually was, for this Reason, that the Table which professes to contain an Account of the Tonnage of Vessels entering the Ports of the United States includes their repeated Voyages, so that the Quantity of these different Descriptions of Tonnage really existing, must be much less than it appears to be in the Table.—It is proper further to observe, that many British Ships may have entered the Ports of the United States without having directly cleared out for the said Ports from

meafures, hitherto adopted by the faid Government, as can have any influence on the Commerce and Navigation of the Britifh dominions.

A Con-

---

from any Britifh Port, or without returning directly from the faid Ports to a Britifh Port; and in fuch cafe, they would not appear in the Accounts furnifhed by the Offices of Government from which the Averages ftated in the Report were taken. It is a known Fact, and is ftated as fuch in the Report, that many Britifh Ships are employed in carrying on a direct Commercial Intercourfe between the Countries belonging to the United States and Foreign European Nations, and return only occafionally to a Britifh Port.

The foregoing Obfervations are fufficient to account for many of the Differences that will be found between the Accounts of Tonnage given in the faid Table, and the Average Accounts of Tonnage ftated by the Lords of the Committee of Privy Council in their Report, which were taken either from Accounts furnifhed by the Public Offices of this Kingdom, or from Information they had previoufly received from America.

The great Superiority, which Britifh Navigation enjoys in the Commerce with the United States, is no lefs evident from the Accounts ftated in the foregoing Table, than from the Averages ftated in the Report of the Committee. The Quantity of the Tonnage of Britifh Veffels which entered the Ports of the United States in the Period to which this Table refers, appears thereby to be more than Three Sevenths of the Tonnage of all the Veffels belonging to the United States, whether employed in their Over-Sea Trade, their Coafting Trade, or their Fifheries : It appears to be even more than Three Fifths of all the American Tonnage employed in their Over-Sea Trade, which is the only Branch of the Trade with the United States in which Britifh Ships are allowed to have a Share, and to enter into Competition with the Ships of the faid States.—The Tonnage of the Veffels belonging to all other European Nations entering the Ports of the United States, as ftated in the Table, during the Period to which it refers, is in Quantity but little more than that ftated in the Report of the Committee; and it would probably not exceed the faid Quantity, if we had Data fufficient to enable us to make the proper Deductions; but

H

compared

A Convention of Delegates, deputed from all the States compofing the United States of America, affembled at Philadelphia on the 17th day of September 1787.—This Convention agreed upon a certain number of fundamental Articles, which were to form the bafis of the new Conftitution, and laid them before the Congrefs of the United States, then affembled, advifing that thefe fundamental Articles fhould be fubmitted to a Convention of Delegates chofen in each Individual State by the people thereof, under the recommendation of its exifting Legiflature, for their affent and ratification ; and that, as foon as the Conventions of Nine States fhould have ratified the Conftitution, founded on the fundamental Articles before mentioned, and have fignified the fame to the United States in Congrefs affembled, the faid Congrefs fhould appoint the time and place, purfuant to the faid Articles, for commencing the proceedings neceffary to the Formation and Eftablifhment of the new federal Government.

As foon as Nine States had acceded to the Plan before mentioned, the late Congrefs, in purfuance thereof, gave the neceffary orders for

---

compared with the Tonnage of the Britifh Veffels which, according to this Table, entered the Ports of the United States during the fame Period, it is equal only to one-fixth part ; though, according to the Averages ftated in the Report, from Accounts of the preceding Years, it was then fuppofed to be equal to about one fourth.

If Congrefs continue to publifh every Year Accounts of the Tonnage of Veffels entering their Ports, in the fame manner as they have done for the laft Year, we fhall be able in Time to form a more decifive and accurate Judgment on this Subject. ——The Reafoning of the Lords of the Committee in the fubfequent Parts of the Report, is rather confirmed and ftrengthened, than in any degree weakened, by the Accounts ftated in the beforementioned Table.

the

the Election of a Senate and a Houſe of Repreſentatives, of which the new federal Government was to be compoſed. This Senate and Houſe of Repreſentatives firſt began to ſit at New York on the 4th of March 1789. They have already held two Seſſions, and have made ſeveral Laws for regulating the Commerce of the United States: —A new commercial Syſtem therefore is now formed, which it is the intention of this Committee to lay before Your Majeſty.

This commercial Syſtem is founded ; *Firſt*, in the fundamental Articles of the new Conſtitution, as ſettled by the Convention of the 17th September 1787 :—And *Secondly*, in the Laws which the new Congreſs, aſſembled according to this Conſtitution, have paſſed in the two Seſſions already held by them.

By the firſt Article of the new Conſtitution, Section 8, a power is given to the Senate and Houſe of Repreſentatives (which the Committee will in future call the Congreſs) with the Aſſent of the Preſident of the United States, (which Aſſent is to be given by him under certain regulations preſcribed by the ſaid fundamental Articles) to lay and collect, taxes, duties, impoſts and exciſes ; and it is declared, that all duties, impoſts and exciſes are to be uniform throughout the United States.

By the ſame Article, Section 9, No tax or duty is to be laid on articles exported from any of the States ; and no preference is to be given by any regulations of Commerce or Revenue to the Ports of one State over thoſe of another.

By the ſame Article, Section 10, No State, without the conſent of Congreſs, is to lay any duties on imports or exports, except what may be abſolutely neceſſary for executing the laws, called the

H 2   Inſpection

Infpection Laws*; and the net produce of all duties, laid by any Individual State on imports or exports, is to be for the ufe of the Treafury of the United States ;—And all fuch laws are to be fubject to the revifion and controul of Congrefs; and no State without the confent of Congrefs is to lay any duty of Tonnage.

By the fame Article and fame Section, No State is for the future to emit bills of credit, or coin money, or to make any thing, but gold and filver coin, a tender in payment for debts :—And by the fame Article, Section 8, Congrefs is to have a power to coin money, and to regulate the value of fuch coin, and to fix the ftandard of weights and meafures.

By Article 1ft, Section 10, No State is to pafs any *ex poft facto* law, impairing the Obligation of Contracts.

By the fame Article, Section 8, Congrefs is to have a power to eftablifh uniform laws on the fubject of Bankruptcies throughout the United States.

By the fame Article and fame Section, Congrefs is to regulate Commerce with foreign Nations :—And by Article 6, All Treaties made, or which fhall be made, under the authority of the United States, are to be deemed the Supreme Law of the Land ; and the Judges in every State are to be bound thereby, any thing in the Conftitution or Laws of any Individual State to the contrary thereof notwithftanding : And laftly, by Article 3, Section 1 and 2, Congrefs is authorized, from time to time, to eftablifh one fupreme court, and other inferior courts, in which the judicial Power of the United

---

* The Infpection Laws are, Laws paffed by the Legiflatures of the feveral States, for appointing Infpectors to afcertain the Quality of certain Commodities exported.

States

States is to be vested:—And this judicial Power is to extend to all cases in law and equity, arising under the present Constitution, or under Treaties made or to be made by the authority of the United States, and to all cases affecting Ambassadors or other public Ministers and Consuls, and to all cases of Admiralty and Maritime Jurisdiction.

It is evident, that many of these Regulations, which are made fundamental Articles of the new Constitution, took their rise from defects which had been perceived in the former system of Government. These Regulations are founded on principles of Justice; and they are certainly favourable to Commerce in general; and if the present Congress carry them fully into execution, many of the laws made by the Legislatures of Individual States, imposing partial burthens on British Commerce, and British Ships, as before stated, will be *ipso facto* repealed.

In consequence of the Regulation, which declares, that all Treaties, already made, or which shall hereafter be made, shall be deemed to be a part of the Supreme Law of the Land, and that the Judges in every State shall be bound thereby, it may be expected, that British Creditors will now reap the benefit of the 4th Article of the late Treaty of Peace, which stipulates, that " Creditors, on either side, " shall meet with no lawful impediment in the recovery of the " full value in sterling money of all *bonâ fide* debts heretofore " contracted."

By the Regulation, which declares, that no State is to pass any *ex post facto* law, impairing the Obligation of Contracts, all the laws, made by the Legislatures of Individual States, to prevent British

Merchants

Merchants from recovering the full value of their legal debts, muſt be conſidered as *ipſo faſto* repealed.

By the Regulation, which declares, that no State ſhall make any thing but gold and ſilver coin, a tender in payment of debts, and that Congreſs alone ſhall coin money, and regulate the value of ſuch money, as well as of all foreign coin, the Laws, paſſed by the Legiſlatures of Individual States, which oblige Britiſh Merchants to take, in payment of their debts, any thing beſides what is thus made legal tender, muſt be conſidered alſo as *ipſo faſto* repealed.

And laſtly, the Regulation which authoriſes Congreſs to eſtabliſh Judicatures for deciding all ſuits and controverſies ariſing under the preſent Conſtitution, and under Treaties, &c. affords juſt reaſon to expeſt that theſe Fundamental Articles will be carried into complete execution ; and that in all theſe reſpeſts the Legiſlatures of the Individual States, and the Courts of Judicature dependent on them, will no longer have the power of reſiſting, under any pretence, the ſupreme authority of Congreſs.

In a word, many of the injuſtices and partialities, hitherto praſtiſed by the Legiſlatures of particular States, have thus been condemned by the United Voice of the People of America aſſembled in convention ; and it is certainly reaſonable now to expeſt that the preſent Congreſs, which is compoſed of a body of men aſſembled from every part of the United States, and who aſt upon a larger ſcale, and in ſupport of a more extenſive and general intereſt, will not commit the like aſts of injuſtice, to which the Legiſlatures of particular States were too frequently liable, in favour of the immediate and preſſing intereſts of the perſons by whom they were eleſted, and ſometimes

even

even to relieve the diftreffes of the very individuals who compofed thefe Provincial Legiflatures.

The Lords of the Committee will now proceed to give an account of the feveral Acts that have been paffed by the prefent Congrefs, in the two feffions already held by them, as far as they relate to the Commerce and Navigation of Your Majefty's dominions.

The principal Acts of this defcription which were paffed by Congrefs in their firft feffion, were the Two referred by Your Majefty to the confideration of this Committee. By the firft of thefe Acts, entitled, " An Act for laying duties on goods, wares and mer-" chandize imported into the United States," the duties on each fort of merchandize, imported into every part of the United States, were made the fame, from whatever country they are brought, and in whatever fhips they are imported, except that a difcount of 10 per cent. of all the faid duties was allowed on fuch goods, wares and merchandize, as fhould be imported in veffels built in the United States, and which fhould be wholly the property of citizens thereof, or in veffels built in foreign countries, and, on the 16th day of May 1789, wholly the property of citizens of the United States, and fo continuing till the time of Importation; and except, that goods imported from China or India, in fhips built in the United States, and belonging to citizens thereof, or in fhips built in foreign countries, and, on the 16th day of May 1789, wholly the property of citizens thereof, and fo continuing till the time of Importation, were made fubject to a lefs duty than the like goods Imported in fhips of the fame defcription from Europe; and except that all the faid laft-mentioned goods, if imported in any other manner, that is, in

fhips

fhips that are not of either of the defcriptions before mentioned, and not directly from China or India, were made fubject to a ftill higher duty.

The particular duties, fo impofed on each fort of goods imported into the United States, will be feen in a copy of the faid Act annexed to this Report *. The Merchants of Glafgow, who have had thefe Duties under their confideration, eftimate that they amount, on an afforted cargo, to $7\frac{1}{2}$ per cent. of its value at moft; and they eftimate the diftinction, made by the difcount of 10 per cent. of the duties, in favour of goods imported in fhips belonging to the fubjects of the United States, to amount, on fuch a cargo, to three-fourths per cent. of its value at moft.

By the fecond of thefe Acts, entitled, " An Act impofing Duties " on Tonnage," a duty was laid on all fhips or veffels built within the faid States, and belonging wholly to the Citizens thereof; and on fhips or veffels, not being built within the faid States, but on the 29th day of May 1789, belonging wholly to the Citizens thereof, during the time fuch fhip or veffel fhall continue fo to belong, - - - - - 6 cents per ton.

On all fhips or veffels hereafter built in the United States, and belonging wholly, or in part, to the Subjects of Foreign Powers - - - - - 30 cents per ton.

On all other fhips or veffels - 50 cents per ton.

On all fhips or veffels employed in the tranfportation of any of the Produce or Manufactures of the United States coaftwife, except fuch fhip or veffel be built within the faid States, and belong to Citizens thereof - - - 50 cents per ton.

---

* See this Act in the Appendix, (C.)

On

On all ships or veffels built in the United States, and belonging to the Citizens thereof, employed in the Coafting Trade, or the Fifheries - - 6 cents per ton, to be paid once in each year.

A *Cent* is the hundredth part of a Spanifh dollar, and in value nearly equal to a halfpenny.

The prefent Congrefs, in their fecond Seffion, repealed the Duties impofed by the firft of the before-mentioned Acts; and, by an Act then paffed, entitled, " An Act making further Provifion for the " Payment of the Debts of the United States," they impofed new Duties, the Amount of which will be feen in a Copy of the faid Act, which is annexed to this Report *.

By this Act, Congrefs have augmented the Duties principally on Wines, Spirits, Teas, Salt, Cables, and Cordage of all forts; and they have augmented them in a lefs degree on fome few Articles of Manufacture, which may be confidered as Objects of Luxury; but on moft other Articles, either of Produce or Manufacture, the Duties are continued the fame †. There is Reafon to believe, that thefe

Duties

---

* See Appendix, (D).

† The Committee have inferted the following Table, in order to fhew on what Merchandizes, and in what Proportions, the Congrefs have thought it right to increafe the Duties of Impoft in the faid Act. It will prove to what Articles the prefent Congrefs principally turn their Attention, when they wifh to increafe the Revenue of the United States by Duties on Goods imported.

				Old Duty.	New Duty.	Increafe of Duty.
				Cents.	Cents.	Cents.
Madeira Wine	-	-	-	per Gall.	18	—	—
London quality	-	-	-	ditto	18	35	17
Other Madeira	-	-	-	ditto	18	30	12

I

All

Duties are carried to the utmoft Extent, which the People of the United States can at prefent bear; for, in the Debates of the Houfe of Reprefentatives,

		Old Duty.	New Duty.	Increafe of Duty.
		Cents.	Cents,	Cents.
All other Wines - - -	per Gall.	10	20	10
Sherry - - - -	ditto	10	25	15
Spirits diftilled Jamaica proof -	ditto	10	—	—
All other Spirits - - -	ditto	8	—	—
If more than 10 per cent. below proof	ditto	8	12	4
If more than 5 and not more than 10 per cent. below proof - -	ditto	8	12½	4½
If of proof, and not more than 5 per cent. below proof - -	ditto	8	13	5
If above proof, but not exceeding 20 per cent. - - -	ditto	8	15	7
If more than 20 and not more than 40 per cent. above proof - -	ditto	8	20	12
If more than 40 per cent. above proof	ditto	8	25	17
Molaffes - - - -	ditto	2½	3	0½
Teas from India.				
In American veffels. Bohea - -	per lib.	6	10	4
Souchong, and other Black Teas -	ditto	10	18	8
Hyfon - -	ditto	20	32	12
Other Green Teas	ditto	12	20	8
Teas from Europe.				
In American veffels. Bohea - -	ditto	8	12	4
Souchong, and other Black Teas -	ditto	13	21	8
Hyfon - -	ditto	26	40	14
Other Green Teas	ditto	16	24	8
Teas from any other place.				
In any other veffels. Bohea - -	ditto	15	15	—
Souchong, and other Black Teas -	ditto	22	27	5
Hyfon - -	ditto	45	50	5
Other Green Teas	ditto	27	30	3
Coffee - - - -	ditto	2½	4	1½

Sugar

fentatives, Complaints have been fince made of the Amount of many of them; and it was on that Account found neceffary not to prefs the immediate Payment of them, on the Delivery of the Merchandize, but to allow longer Credit, than is ufually given to thofe who pay publick Duties; for it appears, that the American Retailer is frequently in Want of Cafh till he has fold the Goods, on which the Duties are to be paid.—A Drawback is allowed of all the faid Duties, with refpect to fuch Merchandizes, as fhall be re-exported within twelve Calendar Months to any Foreign Port or Place, except One per Cent. of the Amount of the faid Duties, which is to

				Old Duty.	New Duty.	Increafe of Duty.
				Cents.	Cents.	Cents.
Sugar	-	Loaf	- -	per lib. 3	5	2
		Brown	-	ditto 1	1½	0½
		Other Sugar	-	ditto 1½	2¼	1
Indigo	- -	- -	-	ditto 16	25	9
Steel, unwrought	-	-		per 112 lib. 56	75	19
Cables	- -	- -	-	ditto 75	100	25
Cordage	- -	{ tarred - -		ditto 75	100	25
		{ untarred, and yarn		ditto 90	150	60
Twine and packthread	-	-		ditto 200	300	100
Coal	- -	-	-	per bufh. 2	3	1
Salt	- -	-	-	ditto 6	12	6
Gold, Silver, and Plated Ware, Jewelery and Paftework - -				ad val. 7½ per ct.	10 per ct.	2½ per ct.
Clocks and Watches	-	-		ditto 5 per ct.	10 per ct.	5 per ct
Coaches, Chariots, &c.	-	-		ditto 15 per ct.	15½ per ct.	0½ per ct.
Glafs	- -	-	-	ditto 10 per ct.	12½ per ct.	2½ per ct.
Paper and Parchment of all Sorts				ditto 7½ per ct.	10 per ct.	2½ per ct.
Marble, Bricks, Tiles, Slates, and other Stones - - - -				ditto 5 per ct.	10 per ct.	5 per ct.
Pictures and Prints	-	- -		ditto 5 per ct.	10 per ct.	5 per ct.
Carpets and Carpeting	-	-		ditto 5 per ct.	7½ per ct.	2½ per ct.
Velvets and Velverets, Cambricks, Muflins, Lawns, Laces, Gauzes, Chintzes, Coloured Callicoes, and Nankeen - - -				ditto 5 per ct.	7½ per ct.	2½ per ct.

I 2

be

be retained as an Indemnification for any Expence, that may have accrued concerning the fame.

In this laft Act, the Congrefs have altered, and in fome degree augmented, the Diftinction made in the Duties on Goods imported in Ships belonging to the Subjects of the United States, or built therein, and belonging in part to the faid Subjects, and on Ships belonging to Foreign Nations; for, inftead of allowing a Difcount of 10 per Cent. of the Duties on all Goods imported in American Ships, as in the firft of thefe Acts, an Addition of 10 per Cent. of the Duties now impofed is made payable on all fuch Goods imported. in any other than American Ships, as before defcribed, except in Cafes, where an additional Duty is fpecifically laid by the laft Act on any Merchandizes imported in fuch Ships.

As the Duties, fo increafed by this laft Act, do not affect many of the principal objects of Britifh Manufacture, they will not probably raife the Duties on an afforted Cargo from Great Britain to more than 1 or $1\frac{1}{2}$ per cent. above what they were in the Act of the firft Seffion, that is, to about $8\frac{1}{2}$ or 9 per cent. in the whole.

The fecond of the Acts referred to the Committee by Your Majefty, entitled, " An Act impofing Duties on Tonnage," was alfo repealed by the prefent Congrefs, in their fecond Seffion; and inftead thereof another Act was then paffed for the like purpofe.

A fhort time after this fecond Seffion commenced, an attempt was made in the Houfe of Reprefentatives to encreafe the Tonnage Duty to one dollar per ton on all foreign-built veffels belonging to

Nations,

Nations, which had not made Treaties of Commerce with the United States; and it was even propofed, that this Tonnage Duty fhould be raifed ftill higher, at fome future period, when the Citizens of the United States had built veffels fufficient for carrying their exports to foreign markets; and that, whenever that period arrived, veffels belonging to Nations, which had not made Commercial Treaties with the United States, fhould not be permitted to export from the Countries belonging to the faid States, any unmanufactured Article, being the growth or produce thereof; unlefs the Nation, to which fuch veffels fhould belong, fhall permit the Importation, into their Territories, of Fifh, and other falted provifions, as well as Grain and Lumber, in veffels belonging to the Subjects of the United States. The Houfe of Reprefentatives came to a Refolution, and ordered a Bill to be brought in, for the purpofes before ftated : This Bill had a firft and a fecond reading; but when it came into the Committee, where it was much difcuffed, the purport of the Bill was wholly altered :—The Diftinction between the veffels belonging to Foreign Nations having Treaties of Commerce with the United States, and thofe that have not, was rejected; and the New Act came out of the Committee, and was afterwards paffed into a Law, impofing the fame Duties, and enacting nearly the fame Regulations, as the Tonnage Act of the laft Seffion.

The prefent Congrefs, in its firft Seffion, paffed an Act for regulating, as well the Collection of the Duties beforementioned, as the manner of entering and clearing out veffels :—This Act was alfo repealed in the fecond Seffion; and inftead thereof a New Act was paffed for the like purpofes.

By this Act, Congrefs have permitted fhips, belonging to the Citizens of the United States, to enter at more ports and places than

fhips

fhips belonging to Foreign Nations :—They have confined the entry of fhips, arriving from any country beyond the Cape of Good Hope, to a certain number of ports therein mentioned, allowing however every fuch fhip to enter at any port, in which fhe may be owned, or from which fhe may have failed on her voyage :—Congrefs have regulated alfo the mode of collecting the Duties *ad valorem*, by enacting, that the value of all fuch Goods fhall be eftimated by adding twenty per cent. to the Invoice price of fuch of the faid Goods, as fhall arrive from beyond the Cape of Hope, and ten per cent. on the Invoice price of fuch of the faid Goods, as fhall arrive from any other Foreign Country.—A difcount of ten per cent. for prompt payment was allowed by the firft of thefe Acts, but it is omitted in the fecond :—This laft Act requires, however, that the Tonnage Duty be paid within Ten Days after the Entry is made, and before the fhip fhall be permitted again to clear out : It is alfo required, that the Regifter of every fuch fhip be lodged, at the time of Entry, in the office of the Collector, and there remain till the time of her clearing out : And it is declared, that no merchandife of Foreign Growth or Manufacture, fubject to the payment of Duties, fhall be brought into the United States in any other manner than by fea, or in any fhip or veffel lefs than Thirty Tons Burthen, except within the Diftrict of Louifbourg.

To enforce the due Execution of the Laws beforementioned, as well as all other Laws, which derive their authority from the Fœderal Government now fubfifting, the prefent Congrefs, in their firft Seffion, paffed an Act for erecting Courts of Judicature for the Trial of all Suits arifing under the New Conftitution, as well as under Treaties, according to the fundamental Article 3d, fection the 1ft and 2d, as before ftated:

By

By this Act, which is entitled, " An Act to eftablifh the Judicial Courts of the United States," Congrefs have created one Supreme Court, to confift of a Chief Juftice and five affociated Juftices : And in each of the Thirteen Diftricts (into which the States are divided for this as well as other purpofes) They have eftablifhed a Court, to be called " The Diftrict Court," in which one Judge is to prefide, who is to be called, " The Diftrict Judge."—They have claffed the Diftricts into Three Circuits, and have appointed a Court in each Circuit, to be called " The Circuit Court," which is to confift of two of the Juftices of the Supreme Court, and the Judge of the Diftrict where they fit.

The Supreme Court is to be holden twice a year, on the firft Monday in February, and the firft Monday in Auguft.—The Diftrict Judge is to hold four Seffions in the year.—The Circuit Courts are to be holden twice a year.

The Laws of the feveral States (except where the fundamental Articles of the Conftitution, the Acts of the Congrefs of the United States, or Treaties made with Foreign Powers, fhall otherwife require or provide) are to be regarded in thefe Courts, as Rules of Decifion in Trials at Common Law, in all cafes to which they apply :— Iffues in fact are to be tried by a Jury in all cafes, except thofe in equity, and thofe of admiralty, and of maritime Jurifdiction.

The feveral Cafes, in which thefe Courts have original Jurifdiction, either concurrent or exclufive, are defcribed in the Act : The Supreme Court has original and exclufive Jurifdiction in all Suits and Proceedings againft Ambaffadors, and other publick Minifters, and their domeftic fervants ;—And it has original, but not exclufive, Jurifdiction, in all Suits brought by Ambaffadors or other publick Minifters, or in which

a Conful

a Conful or Vice Conful fhall be a party : And it has a power to
iffue writs of Prohibition, and writs of Mandamus, in cafes war-
ranted by the principles and ufages of Law, to any Courts appointed,
or perfons holding office under the authority of any of the United
States : There are alfo in this Act many fpecific provifions for regulating the proceedings of all the Courts appointed by this Act, and for
fupporting the exercife of their refpective Jurifdictions. The prefent
Congrefs, in their fecond Seffion, made no alteration in this Act, except
for the purpofe of extending the provifions of it to the State of North
Carolina, and that of Rhode Ifland ; which States had acceded to the
Fœderal Government between the firft and fecond Seffion of Congrefs.

THE Committee having thus brought into one view, all the materials neceffary to affift them in forming their judgment, They will
now proceed humbly to offer to Your Majefty, their opinion on the
feveral points referred to them by Your Majefty's Order in Council
of the 30th September 1789, and by the Letter of His Grace the
Duke of Leeds, one of Your Majefty's Principal Secretaries of State,
dated the 12th November 1790.

The Committee will confider thefe points under the following
heads :

    Firft———COMMERCE.
    Secondly—NAVIGATION.

They will begin with the Commerce of Export from Great Britain
to the United States.

The Extent and Value of this branch of Commerce has been
already ftated ; and it has been fhewn, that nine-tenths of the
Articles,

Articles, exported from Great Britain to the said United States, are British Manufactures.

It has also been shewn, that goods of the same sort, brought from any foreign European country, and imported into the United States, are now made subject, by the Acts of the present Congress, to the same Duties, from whatever European country they may be brought, or in whatever foreign ships they may be imported.

The Merchants, who have been consulted, do not think that these duties on goods imported into the United States, amounting on an average to between eight and an half and nine per cent of their value, are higher than those, to which British goods, so imported, were made subject by the Legislatures of Individual States before the establishment of the new fœderal Government:—And these duties are much less than the duties payable upon British goods of the like sorts imported into most European countries: They are even less than the duties payable on the like sorts of British goods imported into France and Holland according to the late Treaties of Commerce made with those countries ; Great Britain therefore can have no pretence to complain of the amount of these Duties : The United States are now an Independent Nation, and have an undoubted right to impose Duties of the description before mentioned, either for the purpose of raising a Revenue, or of encouraging the produce or manufactures of their own Territories :—As long as the present Congress shall give no preference in this respect to goods of the like sorts imported from other European countries, Great Britain cannot complain of Injustice, nor has She any reason to apprehend a competition :—The excellence and cheapness of the manufactures of Great Britain, and the Credit, which British Merchants are able and willing to give, will always ensure to them a greater share in the

K   Trade

Trade of Export to the United States, than can be enjoyed by any other European Nation. All new eſtabliſhed countries (and ſuch are the United States) can trade only with thoſe nations, who are able to afford them an extenſive credit, and to incur the riſque reſulting therefrom: If all the Colonies belonging to European Nations in America and the Weſt Indies, were to become Independent, Great Britain would have undoubtedly the greateſt ſhare in the Commerce carried on with them.—Even during the late War, the manufactures of Great Britain found their way in great abundance, by indirect courſes, into the countries of the United States; and, notwithſtanding the price of them was very much advanced by the circuitous mode, in which they were conveyed, great quantities were eagerly purchaſed by thoſe who were then the enemies of Great Britain.

It is not probable that the Commerce of Great Britain will ſuffer conſiderably (at leaſt for a long courſe of years) from any encouragement, which the United States may give to their own manufactures, by laying high duties on thoſe of foreign countries.—In the countries belonging to the United States, that are ſituated to the ſouth of Penſylvania, there are no manufactures whatſoever, except a few articles made of leather, which they are enabled to manufacture from the low price of the ſkins purchaſed by them.—The Legiſlatures of the northern and middle States have paſſed laws for the encouragement of manufactures, and have eſtabliſhed ſocieties for the like purpoſe: The Inhabitants of theſe States manufacture ſome coarſe articles for their own uſe, but very few for exportation.—In the northern and middle States, there is ſome wool, but of an inferior quality, and much dearer than in Great Britain.—In the States of New England, linen of a coarſe ſort has been made; and ſome of it has been exported for the uſe of other States.—In New England and Penſylvania there are many iron works; ſome of them were eſtabliſhed before the late War: and the people of theſe States have manufactured nails and

inferior

inferior forts of iron tools, fo as to diminifh very much the importation of thefe articles from Europe.—In New England and New York,
many forts of houfhold furniture are made, and every kind of
carriage in very tolerable perfection, as well as fome other articles,
the materials of which are principally wood and iron.—In New
England and Penfylvania, attempts have been made to introduce
cotton manufactures; but it appears from the fpecimens, that have
been tranfmitted to the Committee, that thefe manufactures are in
general of the common forts, and much inferior in quality, and
dearer than thofe made at Manchefter.—In Penfylvania, paper-mills
have been erected, in which paper is made of a tolerable quality,
fufficient for their own Confumption, and fome even for Exportation:
And in this State, fugar refineries have alfo been eftablifhed (fome
of them even before the War) with fuccefs: and they are now
endeavouring to draw fugar, from a particular kind of Maple, which
they have in great abundance, and thereby to diminifh the quantity
of fugar imported from the Weft India Iflands.—They brew porter
in Penfylvania, but of a very inferior quality.

From this account of the manufactures, at prefent fubfifting in the
United States, nothing can be inferred, that ought to give the leaft
apprehenfion to the Manufacturers of Great Britain. The people of
all countries, who live in temperate climates, will occafionally
employ themfelves in manufactures for domeftic ufe during the
winter months, or at fuch times, as the Cultivation of their Lands
does not require their attendance: But thefe domeftic occupations
feldom give rife to manufactures of any great Extent. The people
of the United States can apply their Induftry with more profit to the
cultivation of the earth: and it is aftonifhing to what a degree the
Inhabitants of all thefe States prefer agriculture to manufacture:
Immediately after the Peace, great numbers migrated from the

northern

northern States to the fouthern in fearch of new Land, which they could obtain at a cheap rate in the uncultivated countries, that lie at the back of the fouthern States : And of late, ftill greater numbers have reforted, and are ftill reforting to the Interior Parts of the American Continent beyond the Mountains, where fix New Settlements are forming : And the People of two of thefe Settlements are already as numerous as the Inhabitants of fome of the antient States. In all the States, to the fouthward of Penfylvania, the principal Inhabitants are great Landholders, and the inferior Inhabitants, Slaves ; neither of which are likely to direct their Induftry to Manufactures. In countries circumftanced like the United States, the Price of Labour will be always too high to enable them to enter largely into the Bufinefs of Manufactures : and, from the want of capital, they can never afford to give the credit, that is neceffary to obtain a Sale of them in foreign Markets.

From what has been faid, the Committee are induced to think, that, with refpect to this branch of Commerce, there are but two propofitions, which it may be proper for Great Britain to make to the prefent Government of the United States, in any Negotiation for a Commercial Treaty with them.

Firft,—That the Duties on Britifh Manufactures, imported into the United States, fhall not be raifed above what they are at prefent.

It may be of ufe to bind the United States, not to raife thefe Duties, above what they are at prefent, by obtaining an exprefs ftipulation for that purpofe : But if this Conceffion cannot be obtained, it may be fufficient perhaps to ftipulate, that the Duties on Britifh Manufactures, imported into the United States, fhall not at any time

be

be raifed above the Duties now payable on the like Manufactures imported from Great Britain into France and Holland, according to the Commercial Treaties with thofe two Powers: Or at leaft, that thefe Duties fhall not be higher than thofe payable on the like Manufactures imported into the United States from the moft favoured European Nation.

Secondly,—That the Duties on all other Merchandize, whether Britifh or Foreign, imported from Great Britain into the United States, fhall not be raifed higher at any time, than the Duties payable on the like Merchandize imported from any other European Nation.

This equality of Duties is founded in Juftice. Great Britain enjoys it by the Laws of the prefent Congrefs: But it may be of ufe to bind the United States to the obfervance of this rule in future, efpecially as the Legiflatures of the Individual States very frequently departed from this rule before the eftablifhment of the prefent Fœderal Government.

The Committee will, in the next place, confider the Commerce of Import into Great Britain from the United States.

The extent and value of this Branch of Commerce have already been ftated. It has been fhewn, that the annual Imports into Great Britain from the United States have diminifhed on an Average fince the War 843,506*l.*; and that this decreafe is nearly accounted for by the decreafed Import of Rice and Tobacco. The Imports from the United States confift principally of Articles of Food, of Naval Stores, and of Materials of Manufactures. All the Articles fo imported, except perhaps Tobacco and Grain, can be obtained from other Foreign Countries, at as low a price, and in as great perfection.

When

When thefe States were Britifh Colonies, the Government of this country granted them favours on account of its Connection with them, and encouraged the Importation into Great Britain of many forts of merchandize produced by them, by allowing them to be imported, either free of duty, or by making them fubject to lower duties, than were paid on the like articles imported from Foreign Countries. Since thefe countries were declared Independent, Great Britain has continued all the diftinctions, to which they were before entitled in favour of feveral forts of merchandize, except as far as relates to Oil, and the produce of their Fifheries : And in all other refpects, the Imports into this Kingdom from the United States are put on an equal footing with thofe of the moft favoured European Nation, except fuch nations only, with whom Great Britain has made Commercial Treaties, founded on reciprocal advantages. It has been fhewn in a former part of this Report, what the amount of the feveral before mentioned diftinctions is : If they were abolifhed, it is probable that the Imports from the United States would fuffer a ftill greater reduction ; and it may well be doubted, whether any other fufficient market could be found for the fale of many of thofe articles, which are now brought from thence to Great Britain. Even at prefent, great quantities remain on hand after plentiful crops : And this confideration has induced fome perfons to think that the Commerce of the United States will in future decline, unlefs they can produce new ftaples proper for the European market.

Tobacco is at prefent the moft important ftaple of the United States. The Commerce of this Article is ftill of benefit to Great Britain, though the Import of it has been greatly diminifhed fince the War. This diminution is owing to the lofs of the monopoly, which we enjoyed before the War, when the Tobacco of thefe countries could, by the laws then in force, be imported only into Great Britain: and yet by continuing higher Duties on the

Tobacco

Tobacco imported from other countries, Great Britain ftill gives to the United States a monopoly againft herfelf in the Import of this Article. If the Tobacco of all Countries was made fubject, on importation, to equal duties, this commodity would be imported from the Eaft Indies, from the Spanifh and Portuguefe Colonies in America, either through Spain and Portugal, or through the Britifh Iflands in the Weft Indies; and in a fhort time, it would probably be imported from the populous fettlements now forming on the banks of the Ohio and Miffiffipi, where Tobacco of the beft quality is faid to be produced : Great Britain would thereby obtain a greater variety of affortments, and her Trade in Tobacco would be confiderably augmented.

Corn is another Staple Article. It is only in years of general fcarcity that Great Britain has occafion to import from the United States Corn for the confumption of its Inhabitants. At all other times, the furplus quantity, which may be wanted for food, can be obtained, either from Ireland, from the Province of Quebec, or from foreign European countries. It is certainly, however, advantageous to the Commerce of Great Britain, to encourage the importation of Tobacco, Corn, and Rice, and all other articles into this country as a depofit : But it may be doubted, whether we do not counteract this policy, by encouraging the importation of any of thefe articles from the United States, in a manner that difcourages the Import of them from foreign countries. The Britifh Merchant will certainly be able to purchafe all thefe commodities at a cheaper rate ; and thereby to improve his trade in them, by having a greater number of markets, to which he can refort upon equal terms for the purchafe of them.

After mature confideration of the foregoing circumftances, the Committee think that, under this head, there is but one propofition,

to

to which the Government of Great Britain can fafely give its affent in any Negotiation for a Commercial Treaty with the United States, viz.

That no higher duties fhall at any time be impofed by the Britifh Legiflature on any Merchandize, the production or manufacture of the United States, imported from thence into Great Britain, than are now payable on the like article, imported from the moft favoured European Nations, even from France and Holland, according to the Commercial Treaties now fubfifting with thefe powers.

It will not be proper even to make this conceffion, unlefs the United States will, in return. agree to ftipulate, that the Imports into the United States from Great Britain fhall, in like manner, continue on the footing of the moft favoured Nation, as before propofed.

The Committee do not think it advifeable that the Government of Great Britain fhould bind itfelf to continue, even for a limited time, the diftinctions hitherto made in favour of certain Sorts of the Merchandize of the United States, imported into this country. Great Britain may find it for her intereft, in her Negotiations with other Foreign Powers, to make the Duties on Goods imported from thofe Countries the fame, as on the like fort of Goods imported from the United States, either by reducing the Duties now payable on their Importation from other Foreign Countries, or by raifing the Duties now payable on their Importation from the United States. It is not, however, the opinion of the Committee, that the prefent fyftem fhould be difturbed, unlefs in cafes, where it is evident that fome alteration is neceffary for the general Improvement of the Commerce of Great Britain.

The

The Commerce carried on with the United States, confifting for the moft part of an exchange of Britifh Manufactures for Naval Stores, and Raw Materials, is entitled to fome favourable diftinctions, (though not perhaps to the prefent extent), where fuch diftinctions do not interfere with the attention, which Great Britain is bound to pay to other more effential Interefts, or with the Juftice which fhe owes to other Foreign Nations in alliance with her.

It is proper alfo to obferve, that this Commerce is carried on with Britifh Capitals in a much greater degree, than the Commerce carried on with any other Foreign Country; and in all Commercial Matters, the Merchants of Great Britain continue ftill to have a clofe Connection with the Subjects of the United States; fo that any great and fudden Change would be feverely felt by thofe who, under the Faith of the Syftem, adopted by the Britifh Government fince the Declaration of Independence, have engaged again in this Branch of Commerce, and embarked their property in it. Any Change, which may be made, fhould be gradual: And there will be lefs Ground of Complaint, if it can be fo contrived, that without Detriment to the public Revenue, the Duties on Goods, imported from other Foreign Countries, fhould be reduced to the level of thofe, now payable on the like Sorts of Goods, imported from the United States, and that thefe laft Duties fhould in no cafe be augmented.

The Committee will confider in the next place the Commerce carried on by the remaining Britifh Colonies in America and the Britifh Iflands in the Weft Indies, with the countries belonging to the United States.

This Branch of Commerce is certainly diminifhed fince the laft war. The Committee have not been able to obtain an accurate

L

Account

Account of it. The Imports into our Colonies and Iflands from the United States, confift of feveral forts of Provifions,—and of Staves, Lumber, and all forts of Timber fit for building, none of which are fubject to any Duty; and confequently no accurate Account can be obtained of the Quantity of each Sort fo imported: It is evident, however, from the great Diminution in the Shipping employed in this Branch of Commerce, that thefe Imports muft have greatly dimi-nifhed.—The Exports from the Britifh Iflands in the Weft Indies to the United States, confift principally of Sugar, Rum and Coffee.— The following Account will fhew the Quantities of each of thefe Articles annually exported to the United States before and fince the War on an average.

					Before the War. Gallons.	Since the War. Gallons.
Rum	-	-	-	-	2,559,664————	1,653,609
					Cwt.	Cwt.
Sugar	-	-	-	-	46,943————	31,167
					Cwt.	Cwt.
Coffee	-	-	-	-	3,246————	2,063

Though this Branch of Trade has diminifhed both in Imports and Exports, a proportionable Increafe has thereby been produced in the Commerce carried on between the Britifh Iflands in the Weft Indies, and the Colonies remaining to Great Britain in North Ame-rica, and between the faid Iflands and Great Britain and Ireland. This Increafe is evident, from the increafed quantity of fhipping employed in thefe different Branches of Trade, as before ftated. It has already been mentioned that, immediately after the Peace, the Commercial Intercourfe between the remaining Britifh Colo-nies and Iflands, and the Countries belonging to the United States, was regulated by Your Majefty's Order in Council, and

that

that it is now regulated by Act of Parliament. This Commerce, with refpect both to Imports and Exports, is left nearly upon the footing on which it ftood before the War, except that Salted Provifions, and the Produce of the Fifheries of the United States, are not allowed to be imported from thence into the Britifh Colonies and Iflands.

With refpect to this Branch of Commerce, it may be proper for Great Britain to make the following Propofition in any Negotiation for a Commercial Treaty with the United States, viz.

That the Commercial Intercourfe between the remaining Britifh Colonies in North America, or the Britifh Iflands in the Weft Indies, and the Countries belonging to the United States, as far as relates to Imports and Exports, fhould continue on the prefent footing for a limited Number of Years.

The Committee think that it would not be advifeable for Great Britain to enter into any Engagement on this Subject for an unlimited Number of Years. It has been found by Experience, that the Britifh Iflands in the Weft Indies become every Year lefs in want of the Provifions and Lumber, which they have hitherto obtained from the Countries of the United States : And a confiderable quantity of Provifions is now produced in fome of thefe Iflands, particularly in the Ifland of Jamaica.—Both Provifions and Lumber are now fent to a large Amount from Great Britain, as well as from the remaining Britifh Colonies in America, and Provifions from Ireland : And it cannot be doubted, that the Provifions and Lumber, imported from the United States into the Weft India Iflands, tend to diminifh the immediate Intercourfe, as well between thefe Iflands and the Britifh Dominions in Europe, as between the faid Iflands and the remaining Britifh Colonies in America.—Whether it may ever be proper, all circumftances confidered, to put further Reftraints

on

on the Imports from the Countries belonging to the United States into the Weſt India Iſlands, is a point, which it is not neceſſary at preſent to decide. The Policy of Great Britain, in this reſpect, will depend on future Contingencies: but it would be improper, by any Stipulation in a Commercial Treaty, to relinquiſh for ever the Right of taking this Subject into Conſideration, as occaſion may require.

The Committee will now proceed to the Second Head,

NAVIGATION.

The Ships of the United States, coming to the Ports of Great Britain, have hitherto been permitted by the Britiſh Government to continue upon the ſame footing as before the War. They do not pay the Alien's Duty; though the Ships of all other Foreign Nations pay it, as before mentioned: They pay, however, Trinity Dues, Light Houſe Duties, and Pilotage, as Foreign Ships, in all the Ports of Great Britain, except London, where they ſtill continue to pay theſe only as Britiſh Ships.

The only Reſtriction, which the Government of Great Britain has put on the Ships of the United States, ſince the ſaid States were declared independent, is in the Trade carried on by them with the Britiſh Colonies in America, and the Britiſh Iſlands in the Weſt Indies; in the Commercial Intercourſe with theſe Colonies and Iſlands, the Ships of the United States are now treated as the Ships of all other Foreign Nations, and are not allowed to import or export any Merchandiſe whatever.

In a former part of this Report, an Account has been given of the Diſtinctions made, to the Diſadvantage of Britiſh Ships, in the Commerce with the United States, both before and ſince the Eſtabliſhment

blifhment of the new fœderal Government. Thefe Diftinctions confifted, either of higher Tonnage Duties on Britifh Ships than on
other Ships, or of higher Duties on Goods imported in Britifh Ships
than in other Ships. It has been ftated, that the Tonnage Duties,
impofed by the Legiflatures of the feveral States before the Eftablifhment of the new fœderal Government, were, upon an Average, 2 s. 3 d. per Ton more than were impofed on Ships of the
United States: And that the Difference of Duties on Goods, imported in a Britifh Ship, was then 2 per Cent. on their value
more, than the Duties on the like Goods imported in Ships of the
United States: So that a Britifh Veffel of 200 Tons would pay
for each voyage 22 l. 10 s. Tonnage Duty; and for a cargo of the
value of 2,000 l. Sterling, 40 l. Import Duty more than a Ship of
the United States of the fame Tonnage, and laden with Goods of
the fame value.

It has alfo been ftated, that the Tonnage Duty, impofed by the
prefent Congrefs, on Britifh or other Foreign-built veffels, is 2 s. per
Ton more, than is impofed on Ships of the United States; fo that
this Diftinction is lefs by 3 d. per Ton, than was impofed on Britifh
Ships by the Legiflatures of the feveral States, previous to the Eftablifhment of the new fœderal Government.

It has alfo been ftated, that, by an Act of the prefent Congrefs, it
is required that there fhall be paid for the Cargoes, imported in
Britifh or other Foreign Ships, an Addition of 10 per Cent. of the
Duties, payable on the like Goods imported in a Ship of the United
States. The Merchants of Glafgow eftimate this Duty to be $\frac{3}{4}$ per
Cent. on the value of the Cargo, and confequently $1\frac{1}{2}$ per Cent. lefs
than the Diftinction made in this refpect by the Legiflatures of the
feveral States before the Eftablifhment of the new fœderal Government;

ment; fo that a Britifh Ship of 200 Tons will now pay for each Voyage 20 l. Tonnage Duty, and for a Cargo of the Value 2,000 l. Sterling, 15 l. Import Duty, more than a Ship of the United States of the fame Tonnage, and laden with Goods of the fame Value.

The Lords of the Committee have thought it right to bring thefe Facts and Calculations once more under the View of Your Majefty, in order to fhew that the Diftinction in Tonnage and Import Duties, now made between a Britifh Ship, and a Ship of the United States of the fame Burthen, and laden with a Cargo of Merchandife of the fame Sorts and Value, is about Five Twelfths lefs than it was before the Eftablifhment of the new fœderal Government.

There is at prefent no Diftinction between Britifh-built Ships and other Foreign-built Ships.—Ships built in the United States, and owned in part by Foreigners, pay 20 Cents, or 10 d. per Ton lefs Duty than Foreign-built Ships, when they are employed in the Over-Sea Trade, between the United States and Foreign Countries: In the Coafting Trade, Britifh Ships pay the fame Tonnage Duty as other Foreign-built Ships. The Effects produced by the Diftinctions made by the Government of the United States (even when they were five-twelfths more than they are at prefent) upon Britifh and American Navigation, are fhewn in the Table prepared for that purpofe, and inferted in a former part of this Report: It will be there feen, that the Navigation of Great Britain, notwithftanding all thofe Diftinctions, has, upon the whole, greatly increafed fince the War :—It will there alfo be feen that, of Six different Branches of Freight, in which the Veffels belonging to the Inhabitants of the Countries, now forming the United States, had a confiderable Share before the War, there are Five, of which they are now wholly deprived ; And, in the Sixth or remaining Branch of Freight, viz. " in the direct Com-" merce carried on between Great Britain and the United States," they

they retain little more than the fame Proportion they enjoyed before the War, though they have endeavoured, in the manner before ſtated, to favour their own Navigation, and depreſs that of Great Britain.

It is certain alſo, that the Ships of Great Britain enjoy other Advantages ſufficient, in a great meaſure, to compenſate the unfavourable Diſtinctions before mentioned :

Firſt—The Premium of Inſurance on a Ship of the United States, bound to and from America, is much greater than the Premium on a Britiſh Ship :

Secondly—The Difference between the Port Charges of all Deſcriptions, ſuch as Trinity-Dues, Light-Houſe Duties, and Pilotage, paid in the Ports of Great Britain, (though various according to the Ports at which the Ship arrives,) is in every one of them very much in favour of a Britiſh Ship :

Thirdly—The Ships of Great Britain derive a conſiderable advantage from having a more univerſal and extended Navigation, while the Navigation of the United States is more confined, as their Ships are not permitted to trade to the Britiſh Iſlands in the Weſt Indies, and cannot venture with ſafety into the Mediterranean, or to the Southern parts of Europe, for fear of the Barbary Corſairs.

But though theſe Advantages may perhaps compenſate the Diſtinctions made by the United States to the diſadvantage of Britiſh Ships ; yet it does not follow that no meaſures ought therefore to be purſued by the Government of Great Britain in ſupport of the Shipping Intereſt of this Country, ſo as to counteract the unfavourable Diſtinctions to which Britiſh Ships are now ſubject.—As the ſecurity of the Britiſh Dominions principally depends on the greatneſs

of

of Your Majefty's Naval Power, it has ever been the Policy of the Britifh Government, to watch with a jealous eye every attempt, that has been made by Foreign Nations to the Detriment of its Navigation: And even in cafes where the Interefts of Commerce, and thofe of Navigation, could not be wholly reconciled, the Government of Great Britain has always given the preference to the Interefts of Navigation; and it has never yet fubmitted to the impofition of any Tonnage Duties by Foreign Nations on Britifh Ships trading to their Ports, without proceeding immediately to Retaliation.

In the year 1593, during the reign of Queen Elizabeth, the State of Venice, (which was then one of the firft maritime Powers of Europe,) made a diftinction to the difadvantage of Englifh Ships in the Duties on Merchandize imported into, or exported from, the Venetian Territories: Queen Elizabeth, in a Charter fhe at that time gave to the Turkey Company, forbad, for the twelve years, during which the faid Charter was to continue, the Importation into England of Currants, or the Wine of Candia in Venetian Ships, upon forfeiture of the faid Ships and their Cargoes, unlefs the State of Venice fhould think fit to abolifh the diftinction beforementioned to the Difadvantage of the Ships of England:—And in the year 1660, when the Government of France impofed a Duty of 50 Sols per Ton, payable in the Ports of that Kingdom, upon the Shipping of all Foreign Nations, including therein the Shipping of Great Britain, the Legiflature of this Country by the 12th Cha. 2. ch. 18. immediately impofed, by way of Retaliation, a Duty of 5 Shillings per Ton on all Veffels belonging to the Subjects of France, which fhould trade to the Ports of this Kingdom, and enacted, that this Duty fhould continue to be collected as long as the Duty of 50 Sols per Ton, or any Part thereof, fhould be

charged

charged on Britifh Ships trading to the Ports of France, and three months longer.

As a further inducement to the Government of Great Britain to pay due attention to the Syftem of Policy, which the Congrefs of the United States appear now to have in view, the Committee think it right to fuggeft, that, if the Britifh Legiflature acquiefce in the Diftinctions already made by the prefent Congrefs without Remonftrance, the Congrefs of the United States may, in a future Seffion, be encouraged to increafe thefe Diftinctions, fo as to make them, in the end, effectual for the purpofe, for which they are intended. The Houfe of Reprefentatives, in the two laft Seffions of Congrefs, have certainly had fuch a Meafure in Contemplation: In the laft Seffion they proceeded fo far in it, that a Refolution was paffed, and a Bill was twice read for that purpofe: The Members, returned from the Northern States, ftrongly fupported this Meafure; thofe of the Southern States refifted it, as being contrary to their Interefts: The more moderate Members, both of the Senate, and Houfe of Reprefentatives, thought the time was not yet arrived, when they might venture with fafety to take a ftep of this Importance.

Four Modes of Retaliation have been fuggefted to the Committee: *Firft*—It has been propofed to follow the fpirited Example of the Government of this Country in the Reigns of Queen Elizabeth and Charles II.; and with this view to impofe (as by the 12 *Ch.* 2. *c.* 18.) on the Ships of the United States, coming to this Country, a Tonnage Duty equivalent to the Diftinctions made to the Difadvantage of Britifh Ships trading to the Ports of the United States: But it may be doubted, whether the Precedents, which are urged in fupport of this direct Mode of Retaliation, can properly be applied to the prefent Cafe. The Trade, which Great Britain carries on with the

United States, is certainly of a very different Nature from that, which was carried on with the State of Venice in the Reign of Queen Elizabeth, or with the Kingdom of France in the Reign of Charles II. : The prefent Trade of the United States confifts principally of an Exchange of Britifh Manufactures for Naval Stores and Raw Materials :—The Trade with Venice and France, at the Periods before mentioned, was directly the reverfe : Great Britain then imported from both thefe Countries Manufactures or Articles of Luxury, which were paid for principally by Returns in Raw Materials.— The Woollen Manufacture was then the only one we poffeffed : Any Reftraint put on a Trade of this laft Defcription, by way of Retaliation, could, in no Event, be very detrimental to the Interefts of this Country ; it might even operate for its Benefit : But a Reftriction of the Nature before mentioned, put on the prefent Commerce with the United States, would tend to confine this Trade to fo much of it, as can be carried on in Britifh Ships only, or to the Importation of fo much of the feveral Articles of which it confifts, as may be neceffary for our own Confumption, and would prevent their being brought here as a Place of Depofit, at leaft by American Ships.—Thefe Ships would, in fuch cafe, find it their Intereft to carry their Cargoes directly to other Foreign Countries.

It is the Opinion of fome of the Merchants and Ship Owners, who have been confulted, that, even in the prefent State of this Trade, not only the Ships of the United States, but Britifh Ships have too many Inducements to carry thofe bulky Articles to Foreign Ports, inftead of bringing them to the Ports of Great Britain as a Place of Depofit ; and that to this Circumftance it is to be imputed, that our Trade in Tobacco and Rice has fince the War declined in the Manner before ftated : And it is proper to add, that any Meafure which induces the American Merchant to carry his Commodities

ties to foreign Markets, inftead of bringing them to Great Britain, may have the effect of diminifhing, in return, the Export of Britifh Manufactures to the Countries of the United States.

The *fecond* mode of Retaliation is, that a Duty be impofed on all Manufactures or Merchandize laden in the Ports of Great Britain, on board the Ships of the United States, for the purpofe of being carried to the Countries of the faid States, equivalent to the diftinctions made to the difadvantage of Britifh Ships trading to the Ports of the United States.—This Propofition, which is made by the Merchants and Ship Owners of Liverpool, will, if adopted, have this bad effect, that the Manufactures and Merchandize of Great Britain fent from hence to the United States in Britifh Ships, or in Ships of the faid States, will pay, either here, or in America, higher Duties, than will be payable on the like Goods, imported into the United States from other Foreign Countries, in Ships belonging to Subjects of the faid States: and if Congrefs fhould in future raife the Duties on thefe Manufactures and Merchandize imported in Britifh Ships, or fhould make the diftinctions in the Tonnage Duties greater than they are at prefent, it will be neceffary for Great Britain, in purfuing this line of policy, to impofe equivalent Duties on Britifh Manufactures and Merchandize exported in American Ships; fo that, in the end, the Manufactures and Merchandize, fent from this country, might be wholly excluded from the American Market, to the benefit of the Trade of other Foreign Countries.

The *third* mode of Retaliation is, that the Government of Great Britain fhould allow a Bcunty on Britifh Ships, trading to the Ports of the United States, in proportion to their Tonnage and Cargo, equivalent to the diftinctions made to the difadvantage of Britifh Ships trading to the faid Ports. If this Propofition is adopted, the

Legiflature

Legiſlature of Great Britain will be under the neceſſity of raiſing this Bounty on Britiſh Ships and their Cargoes, in proportion as Congreſs ſhall at any time increaſe the diſtinctions already made to the diſadvantage of Britiſh Ships, trading to the Ports of the United States :—And Congreſs will thus have it in its power to impoſe a charge on the Revenues of Great Britain by the very ſame meaſure, which lays a burthen on the Commerce of Great Britain, and increaſes the Revenue of the United States.

The *fourth* mode of Retaliation is, that a Duty be impoſed on the Merchandize of the United States, imported into this Country in Ships of the ſaid States, equivalent to the diſtinctions made to the diſadvantage of Britiſh Ships, trading to the Ports of the United States.—This Propoſition, taken in its full extent, is liable to all the Objections that have been ſtated againſt the firſt mode of Retaliation : Theſe Objections it is not neceſſary here to repeat.

The Merchants and Ship-Owners of Liverpool appear diſpoſed to proceed to immediate Retaliation. They think that this mode of proceeding will lead to a Negotiation, and oblige Congreſs to conſent to reaſonable terms. They alledge, but without ſufficient foundation, that the Act of the preſent Congreſs, which makes a diſtinction, to the diſadvantage of Britiſh Ships, to the amount of 10 per cent. of the Duties payable on goods imported in them, bears harder upon Britiſh Ships, than any of the diſtinctions enacted in the Laws of particular States before the eſtabliſhment of the preſent fœderal Government : And they add, that the diſtinctions before-mentioned will prevent Britiſh Ships from obtaining freights, while there are Ships of the United States ready to receive them.

The

The Merchants and Ship-Owners of London, Briftol and Glafgow are of opinion, not to proceed to immediate Retaliation.—They think, that it will be advifeable to endeavour firft, by Negotiation, to remove the prefent unfavourable diftinctions ; but if Juftice cannot in this way be obtained, that it will be neceffary, in the end, to proceed to Retaliation:—It is clear therefore, that all thefe Merchants look forward, in certain contingencies, to a meafure of this nature. —The Committee thought it right, on this account, to ftate all the modes of Retaliation, which have hitherto been propofed to them, and the Objections which may be urged againft each of thefe Modes.

After mature confideration of this very difficult part of the fubject, the Lords of the Committee will venture humbly to fuggeft, that, if at length it fhall be found abfolutely neceffary, for the fup-port of the Navigation of this Country, to proceed to fome meafure of Retaliation, the beft that can be adopted is—to impofe upon Tobacco and Rice, the produce of the United States, imported in the Ships of the faid States for the confumption of Great Britain, and upon fuch other articles, the produce of the faid States, as can be obtained from other Countries at as low a price, and in as great perfection, imported in the Ships of the faid States for the like purpofe, a higher Duty than fhall be payable on the like articles, imported from thence in Britifh Ships, or from other Foreign Countries—to allow all fuch articles to be imported from the countries of the faid States, for the purpofe of being warehoufed, fubject to the prefent Duties, even in Ships belonging to the United States—and to grant a bounty of 15 s. per hogfhead on Tobacco, imported in Britifh Ships, on being taken out of the warehoufe for exportation.

It will be proper alfo, in fuch cafe, to make the Ships of the United States fubject to the Aliens Duty, in the fame manner as

other

other Foreign Ships.—It is apprehended that this laſt Meaſure muſt at all Events be adopted; for there is reaſon to believe, that other Foreign Nations will not patiently ſubmit to this Diſtinction, if the Ships of the United States continue to be exempted from it: and it would be highly impolitic in Great Britain to give up this Duty in all caſes, as it certainly affords eſſential Protection to the Shipping Intereſt of this Country, in the Trade carried on with ſome of the Northern Nations of Europe.

The Committee think, that the Mode of Retaliation, before ſug-geſted, will effectually anſwer all Purpoſes, for which it is intended; and it is probable that the Members of Congreſs, who repreſent the Southern States, being ſenſible how much it will tend to diminiſh the Sale of their Staple Commodities, will be thereby induced to reſiſt any violent Meaſures, to which the Members of the Northern States might on this Account be inclined; and that a Majority of Congreſs will by this means be brought to conſent to a fair and reaſonable Settlement of this Buſineſs.

The Committee are of opinion, that this Mode of Retaliation will not, in any material degree, injure the Commerce of Great Britain, at the ſame time that it will protect and ſupport its Navigation.—It will not raiſe the Price of the before mentioned Articles, imported from the United States for the Conſumption of this Country, as a ſuffi-cient Quantity may be imported in Britiſh Ships for that purpoſe; and, by encouraging the Importation of the like Articles from other Foreign Countries, it may tend even to diminiſh the Price of them at the Britiſh Market.

It is clear alſo, that this mode of Retaliation will not tend to pre-vent the Importation of any of thoſe Articles from the United States
into

into this Country, as a Place of Depofit, even in the Ships of the faid States : It lays no new Burthens on thefe Articles imported for that Purpofe in fuch Ships; and it propofes to give a Bounty on Tobacco, imported in Britifh Ships, whenever it fhall be taken out of the warehoufe for re-exportation: This meafure may perhaps have the Effect of reftoring the Trade of Tobacco to the flourifhing State, in which it was before the War, when this Commodity was neceffarily brought from the United States to Great Britain, before it could be carried to Foreign Countries.

A Bounty of 15 s. per Hogfhead will probably be fufficient to anfwer the end, for which it is propofed to be given.—The Mer-chants of Glafgow eftimate the Charges of landing and re-fhipping a Hogfhead of Tobacco in the Ports of Great Britain, and the Freight and Infurance of it from Great Britain to the Ports of Holland and Germany, from 15 s. to 20 s. per Hogfhead.

Whether the beforementioned Bounty may not be too heavy a charge on the Revenue of Great Britain, it belongs not to this Com-mittee to decide: They will only obferve that the Importation of Tobacco into Great Britain, fince the War, is about 50,000 Hogfheads lefs than it was before the War.—If it is fuppofed that the Bounty of 15 s. will be paid even on 60,000 Hogfheads, it will amount to 45,000 l. per annum.—But the Merchants of Glafgow alledge, that a Ship of about 200 Tons, going to a Foreign Port, expends therein not lefs, on an average, than 4 or 500 l. in every Voyage, which is a Gain to the Foreign Port, and a Lofs in equal Proportion to the Ports of Great Britain : And it is certain, that the Duties, which are now paid in every fuch Foreign Port upon the Cordage, Sailcloth, &c. employed in refitting the Ship, and on Wines, Spirits, Beer, Cloth, Candles, &c. confumed by the Crew, and by all thofe, to whom this Bufinefs

gives

gives occupation, would, if fuch Ship came to a Britifh Port, be an Addition to the Revenue of Great Britain :—The Merchants alfo obferve, that many of the Seamen, fo employed, are in the end loft to this Country ; for, by navigating from one Foreign Country to another, they acquire Foreign Connections, particularly in America, where the Englifh Language is fpoken, fo that thefe Seamen no longer retain their natural Attachment to this Country.

The mode of Retaliation before fuggefted, and particularly the Bounty before propofed, will probably preferve this Country from another Evil now impending, and likely to be very detrimental to its Navigation. The Committee have been informed, that there are Merchants in this Country, who are employing a part of their capitals in building Ships in the United States for the purpofe of carrying on their Commerce with the United States in fuch veffels, and thereby avoiding the unfavourable Diftinctions, to which Britifh Ships are now expofed.—Though a project of this Nature is not only detrimental, but even hoftile to the Interefts of this Country, it is doubtful, whether any legal Provifion can be devifed, fufficient to prevent it : The only manner, in which it can be effectually prevented is, to make it no longer the Intereft of any Inhabitant of Great Britain to venture his Property in fuch a fpeculation.

In giving their opinion on this fubject, the Committee have thus far principally had in view the direct Navigation between Great Britain and the Countries belonging to the United States.—On the Navigation between the Britifh Iflands in the Weft Indies, as well as the remaining Britifh Colonies in North America, and the Countries now under the Dominion of the United States, the Committee have already made fome Obfervations in the preceding part of this Report : And, in a former Report of the 31ft May 1784, They humbly fubmitted

mitted to Your Majefty their Reafons for not allowing to the Ships of the United States the Privilege of trading to the Ports of Your Majefty's faid Colonies and Iflands. Your Majefty was pleafed to approve of the advice then given :—Many of the Merchants and Planters of the Iflands in the Weft Indies, who formerly refifted this advice, now acknowledge the wifdom of it :—Parliament, by paffing an Act for making permanent Regulations, founded on this Report, have given their fanction to the Syftem of Policy therein recommended :—The great Advantages, which have refulted from this Meafure, appear in the Accounts ftated in the former part of this Report.

After full confideration of all, that has been offered on the fubject of Navigation, the Committee think that there is but one Propofition, which it will be advifeable for the Minifters of Great Britain to make on this Head to the Government of the United States, in any Negociation for a Commercial Treaty between the Two Countries, viz.— That Britifh Ships, trading to the Ports of the United States, fhall be there treated, with refpect to the Duties of Tonnage and Import, in like Manner, as Ships of the United States fhall be treated in the Ports of Great Britain.

If this Principle of Equality is admitted by the Government of the United States, as the Bafis of Negotiation, it will be proper then to confider, whether Ships of the United States, trading to the Ports of Great Britain, fhould not be made fubject to the Aliens Duty, as well as other Foreign Ships ; and in return that Congrefs fhould impofe on Britifh Ships, trading to their Ports, fome Diftinction, equivalent to the Amount of the Aliens Duty ; or whether every Diftinction of this Nature fhould not be abolifhed on both fides.—The Committee have offered, already, fome Reafons,

N

which

which induce them to think, that the firſt of theſe Alternatives
ſhould be adopted.

If Congreſs ſhould propoſe to apply the Rule of aboliſhing all Diftinctions to Trinity Dues, Light Houſe Duties and Pilotage, ſuch a Propoſition cannot be complied with.   Theſe ſeveral ſorts of Charges are
of ancient Eſtabliſhment, and are the Property of private Perſons, or of
Corporate Bodies ; and the Funds, ariſing from them, are, in many
Inſtances, applicable to Public Works or Charitable Purpoſes.—An
attempt to equalize them would affect the Intereſts of many of the
Ports of this Kingdom, and alter their relative ſituations :—In conſideration of the Diſtinction, which Time and Accident have made
in all theſe reſpects, Docks, Magazines, and other Buildings, have
been erected in ſeveral Ports of the Kingdom at the charge of
Individuals : Any Change of this nature would have the effect of
increaſing the great advantages, which the Capital of Great Britain
already enjoys, in carrying on its Commerce, over many of the other
Ports of the Kingdom : And laſtly, if this Favour was granted
to the Ships of the United States, other Nations would be induced
to claim the like Equality, which it is impoſſible to grant, conſiſtently
with the Intereſts of this Country.

If Congreſs ſhould propoſe (as they certainly will) that this
Principle of Equality ſhould be extended to the Ports of Our
Colonies and Iſlands, and that the Ships of the United States
ſhould be there treated as Britiſh Ships, it ſhould be anſwered,
that this Demand cannot be admitted, even as a Subject of
Negotiation : By the public Law of Europe, every Nation has
a right to regulate the Commerce, which it carries on with its own
Colonies, in the Manner that ſhall appear to be the moſt conducive

to

to the Intereft of the Mother Country: In Regulations of this fort, no Foreign Government has any Right to interfere :—This Branch of Freight is of the fame Nature with the Freight from one American State to another; Congrefs has made Regulations to confine the Freight, employed between different States, to the Ships of the United States; and Great Britain does not objeĉt to this Reftriĉtion.—The United States at prefent enjoy all the Rights and Privileges of an independent Nation ; and, as fuch, they now have no pretence to claim the Privileges, which they once enjoyed as Britifh Colonies.

If, in the courfe of this Negotiation, it fhould be propofed to treat on Maritime Regulations, The Committee are of opinion, that the Government of Great Britain may confent to infert in a Commercial Treaty with the United States, all the Articles of Maritime Law, which have of late been inferted in our Commercial Treaties with other Foreign Powers ; except that any Article, allowing the Ships of the United States to proteĉt the Property of the Enemies of Great Britain in time of War, fhould on no account be admitted :—It would be more dangerous to concede this Privilege to the Ships of the United States, than to thofe of any other Foreign Country :—From their Situation the Ships of thefe States would be able to cover the whole Trade of France and Spain with their Iflands and Colonies in America and the Weft Indies, whenever Great Britain fhall be engaged in a War with either of thofe Powers; and the Navy of Great Britain would, in fuch cafe, be deprived of the means of diftreffing the Enemy, by deftroying his Commerce, and thereby diminifhing his Refources.

The Lords of the Committee agree in opinion with the Merchants of London, Briftol and Glafgow, that before any Meafure of an ad-

N 2

verfe

verfe Nature is adopted, it is proper, that Attempts fhould be made
by Negociation to induce the Congrefs of the United States to confent to fome fair and equitable Plan of Accommodation, and to a
liberal Syftem of Commerce and Navigation, founded on reciprocal
Advantages.—It has been fhewn, in a former Part of this Report,
that, from the Time that Peace was concluded, and that the United
States were acknowledged by Treaty to be independent, the
Government of this Country have never taken any hoftile Step
to mark their Refentment on account of the many oppreffive,
and even unjuft Laws, to which the Merchants of Great Britain
were made fubject by the Legiflatures of the feveral States, previous
to the Formation of the prefent Fœderal Government.—After an
angry Conteft of feven Years continuance, it was not to be fuppofed, that all Refentment would at once be extinguifhed in the
Minds of the People of the United States: In fuch a State of
things, Forbearance, on the Part of Great Britain, in every thing
not effential, was a prudent, as well as dignified Line of Conduct:
There was reafon to hope, that the Spirit, which had produced
many of the beforementioned Acts of Commercial Hoftility, would
in time fubfide, and that ancient Habits, and the Recollection of
former Connections, might bring back the People of thefe States to
a more favourable Difpofition to Great Britain:—Circumftances
might alfo occur, which would tend to detach them from their new
Connections, and make the People of the Two Countries, though no
longer Fellow-fubjects, Friends at leaft, as they were before the
War:—The Government of Great Britain has not been wholly
miftaken in its Expectations:—The new Syftem adopted by the
Congrefs, is certainly much more favourable to the Navigation and
Commerce of this Country, than that, which fubfifted under the
Laws of particular States; and there can be no doubt, from the
proceedings of Congrefs already ftated, and from all that paffed in
their

their Debates during the Two laft Seffions, particularly in the American Senate, that a Party is already formed in favour of a Connection with Great Britain, which, by Moderation on our Part, may perhaps be ftrengthened and increafed, fo as to bring about in a friendly way, all the Objects we have in view.—It would indeed be extraordinary, if, after having fubmitted for the laft feven years to a fituation more difadvantageous than the prefent, the Government of Great Britain fhould at once proceed to Acts of Retaliation, or Commercial Hoftility, juft at the Time that the Powers, who now govern the United States, appear to be more favourably difpofed to this Country :—On the other hand, it would be imprudent to place, as yet, too much Confidence in the fuppofed Intentions of the new Government, till we have learned from Experience, whether Congrefs is likely to perfift in the Principles, it has hitherto adopted, and will have Influence or Power fufficient to carry the Laws, founded on thefe Principles, into Execution, through all the different States.

For thefe Reafons, the Committee are inclined to think, that it may be advifeable for Your Majefty to confent to open a Negociation with the United States for the purpofe of making a Commercial Treaty, efpecially as Congrefs appears inclined to this meafure : But it will be right, in an early Stage of this Negociation, explicitly to declare, that Great Britain can never fubmit even to treat on what appears to be the favourite Object of the People of thefe States, that is, the Admiffion of the Ships of the United States into the Ports of Your Majefty's Colonies and Iflands : It may be proper alfo to make them underftand, that Great Britain has Meafures in view, fufficient for the Protection and Support of its own Commerce and Navigation, in cafe Congrefs

grefs fhould proceed to make further Diftinctions to the Detriment of thefe Important Objects, and fhould refufe to confent to a fair and equitable Plan of Accommodation. The proper Mode of Retaliation, which, in fuch an Emergency, may be purfued, has already been ftated.

There can be no Doubt, that the Commercial Intercourfe which at prefent fubfifts between Great Britain and the United States, is highly beneficial to both Countries; but it is equally certain, that the United States have much more to apprehend from any Interruption of this Intercourfe, than Great Britain has to apprehend from any Reftriction, which the Government of the United States may put upon it:—It has been fhewn, that the Commerce of thefe States with the other Nations of Europe has hitherto been of no great Extent; and there are Circumftances, which make the further Augmentation of it very difficult:—It has been fhewn alfo, that the Merchants of Great Britain alone are inclined to run the Rifk, and to give the Credit, which are effential to the Support of a Commercial Connection with all newly eftablifhed Countries:—The Articles which the People of the United States now fend to the European Markets are but few, and can be obtained in equal Perfection from other Countries: And it is more likely, that the Demand for them from thence fhould in future diminifh, than increafe:—When the Crops of Grain in Europe happen at any Time to fail, the People of the United States will have an Opportunity of exporting (as in the courfe of laft year) great Quantities of Corn to the Markets of Europe; but there is no Trade fo precarious as that of Corn; and no Syftem of Foreign Commerce, permanently profitable, can be founded upon it; and new Settlements are forming in the Neighbourhood of the United States, which will foon rival them in this, and in every

other

other Staple Commodity, which they produce :—The Fisheries of
the United States, once so prosperous, are now greatly declined, because there is no longer any sufficient Market for the sale of the Produce of them ; the former Success of these Fisheries is principally to
be imputed to the Share, which the Produce of them had before the
War in the Markets of the British Dominions :—Since the Peace, the
Merchants of the United States have endeavoured, by means of the
Cheapness of the Rum, distilled from Molasses, to carry on a Trade
to the Coast of Africa, but with little Success :—At the same Time,
They launched also into a Trade with the Countries to the East of
the Cape of Good Hope, particularly China, which was at first profitable ; but this Trade soon found its Limit, and has of late very
much declined ; the People of the United States have not Wealth
sufficient to support any large Consumption of Asiatic Luxuries, so
that those, who have engaged in this Trade, now found their Hopes
on the Profits to be derived from smuggling these Articles into other
Countries :—It must be acknowledged, that the Commercial Intercourse between the United States and the French Islands in the West
Indies has of late been greatly increased ; and it is also probable,
that the Merchants of these States have found Opportunities to open
illicit and profitable Connections with the Subjects of the Spanish
Dominions in America ; but as these Sorts of Commercial Connection, though perhaps encouraged by the People of the French
and Spanish Colonies, are highly detrimental to the Interests of their
respective Mother Countries, and contrary to the Laws, by which
the Commerce of those Colonies has hitherto been regulated, the
Continuance of the Advantages, which the People of the United
States may derive from these Sources of Wealth, must be precarious,
and will depend on Circumstances.—Such is the present State of the
Commerce of the United States ; the Lords of the Committee have
thought

thought it right thus to collect thefe Confiderations, which have
been ftated more at large in the former Parts of this Report, and to
bring them once more under the view of Your Majefty, in order to
fhew that Your Majefty may fafely refift any unreafonable Preten-
fions, but not to prevent a Commercial Arrangement with the United
States, founded on Terms which are confiftent with the effential Interefts of the Commerce and Navigation of the Britifh Dominions.

Accounts received since the Report was printed, with Observations on them.

FIRST ACCOUNT.

THE following Abstract of the Exports from the Countries belonging to the United States of America, from August 1789 to the 30th September 1790, was received after the foregoing Report was printed.—It contains an Account of the Exports from the said States for about thirteen Months, amounting in Value to 20,415,966 Dollars 84 Cents, which, estimating the Dollar at 4 s. 6 d. is equal to £ 4,593,592 Sterling.—For twelve Months, or one Year, the Export therefore would amount to £ 4,240,239.—But the Amount of the Exports from the United States for this Year, is probably considerably more than in a common Year.—The great Want of Grain in Europe during the latter Part of the Year 1789 and the Beginning of 1790, occasioned a vast Export of Grain from the Territories of the United States, so as to raise the Price of Wheat and Flour in those Countries to nearly double, what it is in an ordinary Year.— The great Increase of Exports from the United States during the beforementioned Period is proved by the State of the Exchange.— The Par of Exchange with Philadelphia is 66$\frac{2}{3}$ per Cent. From the Year 1783, this Exchange had been, upon an Average, at about 70, which is between 3 and 4 per Cent. above Par. From November 1789, when the great Export of Grain commenced, the Exchange began to fall, first to 50, than to 45; and, at last, to as low as 40; because there were then Bills on this Country in great Plenty, and the Balance of Trade between Great Britain and Philadelphia (which is usually in Favour of Great Britain) was, during that Period, in favour of Philadelphia, owing to the unusual Export of

O

Grain :

Grain : But in the Month of July 1790, when the Export of Grain from the United States began to decline, the Exchange rofe again to Par, and is likely foon to be above Par, as it was before November 1789.

It appears, by this Abftract, that the Exports from the United States to the Dominions of Great Britain are nearly one Half of the Whole of their Exports.—To the Dominions of France, the Exports of the United States during this Period were lefs than one Half of the Exports to the Dominions of Great Britain ; and it is probable, that the Increafe of the Exports to the French Dominions, above the Common Average, was greater during this Period, than the Increafe of the Exports to Great Britain, or to any other Country, as the Dearth of Corn in the Years 1789 and 1790 affected France much more than any other European Nation. It was lefs felt in Great Britain than in any Country, with which the United States have a Commercial Intercourfe.—About this Period alfo, the Government of the French Iflands, by Regulations of their own, firft opened their Ports, almoft without Reftriction, to the Importation of Lumber, Fifh, Grain, Live Stock, and Provifions, from the United States, contrary to the Interefts and Intentions of the Mother Country.—It appears, that the Value of the Lumber, Fifh, Grain, Live Stock, and Provifions, exported from the United States during this Period, amounted to 10,968,049 Dollars, or £ 2,467,811 : o : 6 Sterling, being more than one Half of the Whole of their Exports.

It is fingular, how fmall the Value is of the Produce of the Whale Fifhery exported from the United States : It amounts only to 252,591 Dollars, or £ 56,832 : 19 : 6 Sterling.

This Abftract does not diftinguifh the Exports to the feveral Nations of Europe, from the Exports to their refpective Colonies ; fo that it is impoffible to determine what Proportion the firft bears to· the latter.

*Letter from the Secretary of the Treasury of the United States,
transmitting to the House of Representatives an Abstract of the
Exports of the United States from August 1789 to the 30th of
September 1790.*

                                      " TREASURY DEPARTMENT,

" S I R,   " February 15, 1791.

      " I DO myself the Honor to transmit through you to the House
" of Representatives, a general Return of the Exports of the United States,
" abstracted from Custom-House Returns, commencing on the various
" Days in August, 1789, whereon they were respectively opened, and
" ending on the 30th of September last. From inadvertence in some of
" those Offices, the Space of Time prior to the 1st of October, 1789, was
" blended with the Quarter following, which prevented an uniform Com-
" mencement of this Abstract on that Day; and there is yet a Deficiency
" of many of the Returns for the last Quarter of the Year 1790, which
" confines the Abstract to the 30th of September last. The Progress which
" was made in this Form of Statement of the Exports, prior to the Order
" of the House, and the Impossibility of having it completed in the Form
" directed by them before the fourth of March next, have occasioned me
" to offer it in its present Shape.

                " I am, &c.

                     " ALEXANDER HAMILTON,
                           " Secretary of the Treasury.

" To the Honorable the SPEAKER
  " of the House of Representatives of the United States."

ABSTRACT of the EXPORTS of the UNITED STATES, from the Commencement of the CUSTOM-HOUSES in the feveral States, which were at different Times in Auguft, 1789, to the 30th Day of September, 1790.

Species of Merchandize, EXPORTED.			Quantity.	Value.
				Dollars. Cts.
ASHES Pot,	-	tons	7,050 : 10	661,634
Afhes Pearl,	-	do.	1,548 : 55	177,459 : 50
Apples,	-	barrels	5,898	6,318
Boats,	-	-	8	372
Bomb Shells,	-	tons	10	100
Bricks,	-	-	870,550	2,617 : 50
Beer and Porter,	-	cafks	472	4,612
Brandy,	-	do.	97	3,016
Cordials,	-	boxes	236	637
Cordage,	-	-		5,739
Carriages,	-	-	220	28,017
Candles Tallow,	-	℔s.	149,680	14,876
Candles Wax,	-	do.	5,274	2,461
Candles Myrtle,	-	do.	249	52
Cyder,	-	barrels	442	849
Cotton,	-	bales	2,027	58,408
Coffee,	-	℔s.	254,752	45,753
Chocolate,	-	do.	29,882	3,537
Cocoa,	-	do.	10,632	950

Species of Merchandize, EXPORTED.	Quantity.	Value.
		Dollars. Cts.
Caſſia and Cinnamon, do.	9,392	9,715
Deer Skins, - -	-	33,009
Duck American, - bolts	77	777
Duck Ruſſia, - do.	220	2,200
Earthen and Glaſs Ware,	-	1,990
Eſſence Spruce, boxes	115	600
Flax Seed, - caſks	40,019	236,072
Flax, - - ℔s.	21,970	1,468
Furs, - -	-	60,515
Furniture, - -	-	8,351
FISHERY.		
Fiſh dried, - quintals	378,721	828,531
Fiſh pickled, - barrels	36,804	113,165
Oil Whale, - do.	15,765	124,908
Oil Spermaceti, - do.	5,431	79,542
Candles do. - ℔s.	70,379	27,724
Whale-Bone, - do.	121,281	20,417
GRAIN.		
Buck-Wheat, - buſhels	7,562	2,572
Corn, - do.	2,102,137	1,083,581
Oats, - -	98,842	20,900
Rye, - do.	21,765	13,181
Wheat, - do.	1,124,458	1,398,998

Species of Merchandize, EXPORTED.		Quantity.	Value.
			Dollars. Cts.
Genſeng, - -	caſks	813	47,024
Gun-Powder, -	℔s.	5,800	861
Gin, -	gals.	18,025	16,989
Grindſtones, -	-	203	450
Hair-Powder, -	℔s.	12,534	1,687
Hats, -	-	668	1,392
Hay, -	tons	2,126	12,851
Horns, -	-	-	1,052
Ironmongery, -	-	-	7,878
Iron Pig, -	tons	3,555	91,379
Iron Bar, -	do.	200	16,723
Indigo, - -	℔s.	612,119	537,379
LIVE STOCK.			
Horned Cattle, - -		5,406	99,960
Horſes, - -		8,628	339,516
Mules, - -		237	8,846
Sheep, - -		10,058	17,039
Hogs, - -		5,304	14,481
Poultry, -	doz.	3,704	6,263
LUMBER.			
Staves and Heading, -		36,402,301	463,229
Shingles, -		67,331,115	120,151

Species of Merchandize, EXPORTED.	Quantity.	Value.
		Dollars.　Cts.
Shook Hogsheads, －	52,558	32,002
Hoops, － －	1,908,310	19,598
Boards, － －	46,747,730	260,213
Handspikes, · doz.	2,361	1,505
Casks, － －	2,423	3,697
Scantling, － feet	8,719,638	95,308
Lumber of different Kinds, do.	-	128,503
Timber of ditto, － do.	-	139,328
Leather, － ℔s.	22,698	5,302
Logwood, － tons	264	3,911
Lignumvitæ, － do.	176	1,760
Lead and Shot, － do.	6	810
Mahogany, － －	-	18,531
Medicine and Drugs, －	-	1,735
Merchandize, － －	-	28,156
Molasses, － gallons	15,537	3,904
Muskets, － －	100	500
Nankeens, － bales	11	2,315
Oil Linseed, － barrels	119	1,962
PROVISIONS.		
Flour, － barrels	724,623	4,591,293
Bread, － ditto	75,667	209,674

Species of Merchandize, EXPORTED.		Quantity.	Value.
			Dollars. Cts.
Meal,	- ditto	99,973	302,694
Peas and Beans,	bushels	38,752	25,746
Beef,	- barrels	44,662	279,551
Pork,	- ditto	24,462	208,099
Hams and Bacon,	℔s.	253,555	19,728
Butter,	- firkins	8,379	48,587
Cheese,	- ℔s.	144,734	8,830
Potatoes,	- barrels	5,318	6,009
Tongues,	- do.	641	1,598
Onions, Vegetables,	-	-	22,936
Hogs Lard,	- firkins	6,355	31,475
Honey,	- do.	165	990
Oysters pickled,	- kegs	272	272
Pimento,	- bags	715	4,928
Pepper,	- ℔s.	6,100	1,440
Paper,	- reams	169	381
Paint,	- ℔s.	4,650	963
Pitch,	- barrels	8,875	17,488
Raw Hides,	-	230	485
Raw Silk,	- ℔s.	177	489
Rosin,	- barrels	316	778
Rice,	- tierces	100,845	1,753,796

Species of Merchandize, EXPORTED.		Quantity.	Value.
			Dollars. Cts.
Rum American,	gallons	370,331	135,403
Rum West-India,	ditto	12,623	5,795
Raisins, - -	casks	213	1,205
Salt, -	bushels	31,935	8,236
Sago, - -	℔s.	2,319	455
Soap, -	boxes	597	3,967
Snuff, -	℔s.	15,350	5,609
Seeds and Roots, - -		-	2,135
Shoes and Boots, -	pairs	5,862	5,741
Saddlery, - -		-	5,541
Starch, - -		-	1,125
Sugar Loaf, -	℔s.	16,429	3,432
Sugar Brown, -	do.	33,358	2,237
Saffafras, -	do.	49,504	555
Steel, -	bundles	163	978
Stones sawed, -		170	550
Tallow, -	℔s.	200,020	20,722
Tobacco, -	hhds.	118,460	4,349,567
Tea -	chests	1,672	121,582
Tar, -	barrels	85,067	126,116
Turpentine, -	do.	28,326	72,541
Ditto Spirits, -	do.	193	1,032

P

Species of Merchandize, EXPORTED.	Quantity.	Value.
		Dollars. Cts.
Tow Cloth, - pieces	67	1,274
Vinegar, - cafks	24	106
Wines, - pipes	1,074	83,249
Wax, - ℔s.	231,158	57,597
		20,194,794
To the North-weſt Coaſt of America - -		10,362
Amount of ſeveral Returns received ſince the 15th February, 1791, - - }		210,810 : 84
	Total,	20,415,966 : 84

RECAPITULATION.

	Dollars. Cts.
Proviſions, - -	5,757,482
Grain, - -	2,519,232
Fiſh, - -	941,696
Lumber, - -	1,263,534
Live Stock, - -	486,105
	10,968,049
Other Articles, - -	9,447,917 : 84
	Total, 20,415,966 : 84

A SUMMARY of the Value and Deſtination of the EXPORTS of the UNITED STATES, agrecably to the foregoing Abſtract.

	Dollars.	Cts.
TO the Dominions of France,	4,698,735	48
To the Dominions of Great-Britain,	9,363,416	47
To the Dominions of Spain,	2,005,907	16
To the Dominions of Portugal,	1,283,462	
To the Dominions of the United Netherlands,	1,963,880	9
To the Dominions of Denmark,	224,415	50
To the Dominions of Sweden,	47,240	
To Flanders,	14,298	
To Germany,	487,787	14
To the Mediterranean,	41,298	
To the African Iſlands and Coaſt of Africa,	139,984	
To the Eaſt-Indies,	135,181	
To tbe North-Weſt Coaſt of America,	10,362	
	20,415,966	84

IN Addition to the foregoing, a conſiderable Number of Packages have been exported from the United States, the Value of which, being omitted in the Returns from the Cuſtom-Houſes, could not be introduced into this Abſtract.

TREASURY DEPARTMENT, *February* 15th, 1791.

TENCH COXE, *Aſſiſtant Secretary.*

P 2

SECOND ACCOUNT *received since the Report was printed.*

THE following Account (which is publifhed by Mr. Jefferfon, Secretary of State to the United States of America, in the Appendix to his Report of the 1ft February 1790, on the Cod and Whale Fifheries, carried on by the Subjects of the faid States) has alfo been received fince the foregoing Report was printed.—It contains an Account of the Quantity of Rice, Flour, Wheat, Rye, and Barley, imported into the Ports of France from the United States of America, in the Year 1789; being a Part of that Period, in which a Dearth prevailed in France, for Want of Provifions of this Nature.—This Account being only for the Year 1789, does not correfpond in Point of Time with the preceding Abftract of Exports from the United States, which contains an Account of the faid Exports from Auguft 1789, to the 30th September 1790.—If the Periods, to which thefe two Accounts refer, had been the fame, it would have been poffible to have ftated with Accuracy, what Proportion of the Whole of thefe Articles, which appear by the firft of thefe Accounts to have been exported from the Countries of the United States, were imported, according to the fecond of thefe Accounts, into the Ports of France. But though thefe Periods are in Part different, it has been thought right to add, at the Foot of this Account, a comparative State of the Quantities of each of thefe Articles exported from the United States, in the Period to which the firft Account refers; and of the Quantities of each of the faid Articles which were imported into

the

the Ports of France, in the Period, to which the fecond of thefe Accounts refers. It will ferve to fhew, generally, how large a Proportion of the feveral Sorts of Grain, exported from the United States, was fent to France, during the Time that there was fo great a Want of them in the Markets of Europe.

It is proper to obferve, that as the Produce of the feveral Sorts of Grain in France is fuppofed to be, in common Years, fufficient for the Confumption of the Inhabitants of that Kingdom, the Trade of the United States with France, in all thefe Articles, except Rice, muft always depend on the Seafon, and confequently be very precarious.

Grain and Flour imported from the United States of America into the Ports of France, in the Year 1789; from an official Statement.

Articles.	Total exported to France.		
	French Quintals. lb.		Tierces of 500 French Pounds each.
Rice	123,401 69		24,680
			American Barrels.
Flour	256,545 94	equal to	140,959
			American Bufhels.
Wheat	2,015,297 3		3,664,176
Rye	307,390 96		558,891
Barley	260,131 52		520,262

Com-

Comparative State of the Quantities of each of the above Articles exported from the United States, in the Period to which the first Account refers ; and of the Quantities of each of the said Articles imported into the Ports of France in the Period, to which the second Account refers.

Total of the following Articles exported from the United States to all Countries, from August 1789, to the 30th September 1790, according to the first Account.	Articles.	Total of the following Articles exported to France from the United States of America in the Year 1789, according to the second Account.			
Tierces. 100,845	Rice	French Quintals. 123,401	lb. 69	equal to	Tierces of 500 French Pounds each. 24,680
Barrels. 724,623	Flour	256,545	94		American Barrels. 140,959
Bushels. 1,124,458	Wheat	2,015,297	3		American Bushels. 3,664,176
21,765	Rye	307,390	96		558,891
	Barley	260,131	52		520,262

THIRD

THIRD ACCOUNT *received since the Report was printed.*

THE following Account of the Number of Veffels which entered the Ports of France, from the United States of America, in the Year 1789, taken from the before-mentioned Report of Mr. Jefferfon, has alfo been received fince the foregoing Report was printed.—This Account will ferve to prove, what is cautioufly fuggefted in the Report of the Lords of the Committee for Trade and Plantations, viz. That Britifh Veffels have a confiderable Share in the commercial Intercourfe carried on between the United States and the feveral Nations of Europe;—for, according to this Account, the Britifh Veffels, that entered the Ports of France from the United States, are above three Times as many, as the French Veffels, that entered the faid Ports from the United States, in 1789; and are above eight Times more than the Veffels of all the other Nations of Europe, and about One-fourth of the Veffels of the United States, that entered the Ports of France, during that Period.—It is probable, that the Share, which Britifh Veffels have in the Commercial Intercourfe between the United States and other Nations of Europe, to the South of France, is more confiderable than the Share they have in the Intercourfe between the United States and France.

Statement

Statement of the Vessels entered in the Ports of France, from the United States of America, in the Year 1789.

				Vessels.		Tons.
French,	-	-	-	13	-	2,105
Imperial,	-	-	-	3	-	370
English	-	-	-	43	-	4,781
Dutch,	-	-	-	1	-	170
Hanseatic,	-	-	-	1	-	200
American,	-	-	-	163	-	24,173
				224	-	31,799

A P P E N D I X.

(A.)

N° I.

QUESTIONS referred on the 15th October 1789, by the Lords of the Committee of Privy Council, appointed for all Matters relating to Trade and Foreign Plantations, to a Committee of Merchants of the City of LONDON, *and to the Merchants and Ship Owners of* BRISTOL, LIVERPOOL, *and* GLASGOW, *concerned in the Trade to the United States of America.*

QUESTION I.

HAVE the Commerce and Shipping Intereſt of this Country ſuffered by the Diſtinctions, which have been hitherto made by the different Legiſlatures of the States compoſing the United States of America, in the Duties impoſed by them on Britiſh or other Foreign Goods, or in the Duties impoſed on the Tonnage of Britiſh or other Foreign Ships, or American Ships, previous to the paſſing the late Impoſt and Tonnage Act by Congreſs ; and in what reſpect and degree ?

[A]   QUES-

QUESTION   II.

WILL the Commerce and Navigation of this Country be upon a worfe footing under the general Duties impofed by the late Impoft and Tonnage Acts of Congrefs, than they have hitherto been under the Duties impofed by the Legiflatures of the particular States compofing the United States of America ?

QUESTION   III.

IF it fhould be thought proper to fubject Goods, brought in American Ships, to the Duties payable generally on Goods brought in Foreign Ships, from which American Ships only have hitherto been exempted, and further to impofe a Duty on the Tonnage of American Ships coming to this Country, equal to the Difference they have made in their Tonnage Act between American and Foreign Shipping coming to their Ports, that is, forty-four Cents of a Dollar ; would thefe Meafures have the Effect of fecuring to the Shipping of this Country the Share it ought to enjoy in the Trade between Great Britain and the Countries belonging to the United States of America ? or would fuch Meafures be the Means of inducing the Americans to carry their Produce in their own Ships to the Ports of other Countries, inftead of bringing it to thofe of Great Britain ?

QUESTION   IV.

IF this Country fhould now acquiefce in the Diftinctions made by the American Congrefs in favour of their own Shipping, to the Detriment of ours, is there any Security, from the Nature and Circumftances of the Trade between the two Countries, that Congrefs will not be encouraged to encreafe the Duties impofed for this Purpofe, till they have fucceeded in driving our Shipping out of this Trade, though the Duties hitherto impofed may not wholly have that Effect ?

QUES-

QUESTION V.

DO not American Ships at prefent prefer carrying the Produce of America, particularly Tobacco and Rice, to the Ports of other Countries rather than to thofe of Great Britain and Ireland; and to what Caufes is this Preference to be imputed?

QUESTION VI.

DO not Britifh Ships, employed in the American Trade, carry the beforementioned American Produce to Foreign rather than to Britifh Ports? and in what Degree, and to what Caufes, is this Preference to be imputed?

Nº II.

Report of the Committee of Merchants trading from LONDON *to America, in Anfwer to the foregoing Queftions.*

ANSWER TO QUESTION I.

UNDOUBTEDLY, both the Commerce and the Shipping Intereft of this Country did fuffer by the Diftinctions made by the United States in favour of other Foreigners, from the opening of the Trade with the faid States in 1783, until thofe Diftinctions were done away by the Law paffed under the prefent form of Government, which took place on the firft of Auguft 1789. In what degree thefe Diftinctions were made, have been fully fet forth in various Memorials to Adminiftration;—they varied in the different States.

ANSWER TO QUESTION II.

THE Commerce and Navigation of thefe Kingdoms we do not conceive to be on a *worfe* footing by the late impofed Duties on Goods imported, and on the Tonnage of Shipping, than they were under the Laws
of the different Legiflatures of the States.—In fome of the States they
are actually benefited by the new Law of Tonnage impofed under the
prefent form of Government.

ANSWER TO QUESTION III.

THE Right of Government to bring forward the Duties payable in general on Goods brought hither in American Bottoms, as are paid by other
Foreigners, cannot be denied; but it is fubmitted, whether the Impofition
of thefe Duties (laying dormant as they have for years paft) fhould not be
difpenfed with yet for a time. The United States are proceeding faft in a
regular form of Government, and the ancient attachment of the people to
this Country gaining ground, they muft wifh and feek a Treaty with us,
when it appears probable Advantages would arife by a temporary forbearance.—Were a Duty of Tonnage to be impofed on American Bottoms
arriving in this Kingdom, equal to the difference of Duties on Shipping
laid in the United States between their own Navigation and ours, it might,
it would for the moment, operate no doubt in our favour, but muft inevitably foon be retaliated by America, who would have an equal right to
difcriminate and lay an overbalance of Tonnage Duty on the Shipping of
thefe Kingdoms.—The difference in favour of our Shipping in the Ports
of America, and what American Shipping pay here, is already confiderable.

An

An American Ship of 160 Tons pays	£.	s.	d.
Light Money - - - - -	21	15	0
Trinity Dues - - - -	5	4	2
Entry inward and outward, and clearing - -	8	7	0
	35	6	2
But 9d. per Ton pierage laid on the Cargo is again reftored to the Ship - - - -	6	0	0
	29	6	2
A Britifh Ship of the fame Burthen in the Ports of the United States, 50 Cents per Ton, equal to 2 s. 3 d.	18	0	0
Entry inward and outward, and clearing, not more than	2	0	0
	20	0	0

Befides this difference in favour of Britifh Shipping, Pilotage, and other Port Charges, are much lefs in America than they are in the Port of London.—Britifh Shipping enjoy a very confiderable fhare of the carrying Trade, particularly from Maryland, Virginia, and South Carolina, nearly to the exclufion of other Foreigners; and tis more than probable, fhould this Country lay a heavier Duty of Tonnage on the Shipping of America, it would be productive of the very meafure fuggefted by the Queftion,—" be the " means of inducing the American Government to caufe their Produce to " be carried in their own Ships to the Ports of other Countries, inftead of " bringing it to thofe of thefe Kingdoms."

ANSWER TO QUESTION IV.

THE Duties hitherto, or at prefent, impofed on Britifh Shipping and on Britifh Goods by the United States, we find, by experience, have not produced the effect of driving the former out of the Trade between the two Countries.—America, in laying her new Impofts, makes no difcrimination to the prejudice of our Shipping, which heretofore fhe did to a confiderable degree: but that partiality to other Foreigners being now extinct, America

would

would no doubt feel much irritated at any *new* Impofitions on the part of this Country; and fhe certainly has it in her power to retaliate. We fhould not complain of the partiality of America to their own Navigation, fince Great Britain fets her the example. If the fubmiffión of Government, without remonftrance on the bufinefs, in the diftinction now made by the United States in favour of their own Shipping, may be called acquiefcence in the meafure, it is not poffible to fay how this filence may hereafter ope-rate, and induce America to increafe the Duties already impofed on Britifh Goods and Shipping: but it is conceived it would not have that effect.

ANSWER TO QUESTION V.

AMERICAN Ships affuredly do prefer carrying the Produce of the United States to the Ports of other Countries; the Caufe feems clear—ex-pectation of better markets,—fhorter voyages;—but one great temptation is, much lefs expence on Shipping and their Cargoes.—The Charges on To-bacco and Rice, particularly the latter, in the Ports of this Country, are feverely felt, and unqueftionably occafion thofe and other articles to be often carried by American Shipping, as well as our own, to foreign Ports. To invite them to thofe of her Kingdom, France gives great indulgencies. —Free Ports, both in the Bay, and in the Englifh Channel, where the con-tingent charges are alfo fmall.

ANSWER TO QUESTION VI.

THIS Queftion may be anfwered nearly as the preceding; Britifh Ship-ping, like all others, unlefs in particular cafes, prefer going to thofe places where the Port Charges are eafy.—The proportion of Britifh Ships, carry-ing the produce of the United States to Foreign Markets, cannot here be eafily afcertained.—Few American Veffels venture within the Streights of Gibraltar, or in the Track of the Barbary Cruizers;—of confequence, in thefe Voyages, Foreign Ships are employed; and in this, we have no doubt, the Britifh have the preference.

The

The Committee are not fufficiently informed to be able to give fatis-factory Anfwers to the Queftions with refpect to the Out Ports.

By Order of the Committee,

13th November, 1789.

(Signed) EDW. PAYNE, Chairman.

Nº III.

Report of the Merchants and Ship Owners of BRISTOL, *in An-fwer to the foregoing Queftions.*

ANSWER TO QUESTION I.

WHEN America treated Great Britain with thofe impolitic Diftinc-tions of partial Duties and Reftrictions, different from the Goods and Ships of other Nations, (as was the cafe in fome of the Provinces,) our Commerce, and efpecially Shipping, fuffered in a confiderable degree.

ANSWER TO QUESTION II.

THE Commerce of this Country will now be on a better footing under the general Duties impofed by the late Acts of the States United, than under the Duties impofed by the Legiflatures of the particular States, the Impoft being more equal, and alike on all Foreigners; and though the Tonnage Duty is both heavy, and calculated to give a preference in the carrying Trade to their own Ships, yet our Navigation being put upon the fame footing with other Foreign Nations, our fuperiority over other Countries will probably be evinced by our abilities and more extenfive con-nections with America.

A N-

ANSWER TO QUESTION III.

IF Duties are laid by Great Britain upon American Produce brought by their Ships, equal to thofe from Foreign States, together with a Tonnage Duty, equal to the Difference between what is laid on Britifh and their own Veffels in America, it might perhaps increafe the carrying Trade in Britifh Ships, but would manifeftly injure the American Trade to this Country, and induce them to prefer fending their Produce in their own Ships to tne Markets of all other Nations. The Balance of the American Trade is importantly in our favour; and that Balance will increafe, as long as America continues in a peaceable and profperous fituation: We therefore wifh to fee the Trade cherifhed by Government; and are of opinion, it would be more to the Advantage of Great Britain to continue her indulgence to the Returns in Produce made us by America, moft of which are very neceffary to our Manufactures.

ANSWER TO QUESTION IV.

THE fettled Form of Government, which America has now affumed, gives fair ground to prefume, that a Commercial Treaty may foon be negotiated between Great Britain and thofe States, which might be fome fecurity againft any Increafe in the American Duties on Tonnage and Merchandize, with refpect to us. The Advantages of Commerce between two independent States, muft be in fome meafure reciprocal, or cannot be lafting: Our markets are as neceffary to America, as theirs to us. The power we have of Retaliation will therefore awe America, and deter her from exceffive Impofitions on our Trade or Shipping.

ANSWER TO QUESTION V.

THE Articles of Rice and Tobacco, have a greater confumption in other European Markets than England; confequently, the Americans will, from Intereft, prefer carrying direct, rather than by bringing fuch Produce

to

to our Ports, to make Great Britain the Grand Repofitory, where they complain of being fubjeĉt to much Expence, and perplexing Inconvenience, in the difcharging and re-exporting of fuch Cargoes.

ANSWER TO QUESTION VI.

BRITISH Ships, employed in that Trade, prefer carrying American Produce direĉt to other Countries from the fame Caufes; and it is probable, the Severities exercifed under fome of the late Aĉts and Regulations have a Tendency to induce Britifh Ships to prefer Foreign Voyages.

Nº IV.

Report of the Merchants and Ship Owners of LIVERPOOL, *in Anfwer to the foregoing Queſtions.*

ANSWER TO QUESTION I.

THE Commerce and Shipping Intereſt of this Country have undoubtedly fuffered by the Diſtinĉtions, which have been made by the different Legiſlatures of the American States, in the Duties impofed by them on Britifh Ships, by way of Tonnage Duties, and upon Britifh Merchandize, previous to the paſſing of the late general Impoſt and Tonnage Aĉt; inafmuch as American Veſſels have obtained a preference in confequence of them in Britifh Ports, and to fuch a degree, that Britifh Ships could procure no Freights, whilſt American Ships were in the way to receive them, except in the Trade to Penfylvania, where neither Reſtriĉtions nor Diſtinĉtions did exiſt, and Britifh Veſſels had even a decided Preference.

[B]   AN-

ANSWER TO QUESTION II.

THOUGH the Duties impofed by the late Impoft and Tonnage Act of Congrefs may not be higher upon an Average than thofe exacted under the Legiflatures of the different States; yet that Claufe in the late Act of Congrefs, which remits ten per cent. of the Duties upon Wares and Merchandizes imported in American Veffels, bears harder upon Britifh Ships than any thing which exifted in the American Laws before, and will prevent them from obtaining Freights from Great Britain, whilft American Veffels offer to receive them.

ANSWER TO QUESTION III.

IT is believed, that a Duty upon Goods imported from America in American Ships to Great Britain would not be found to anfwer the Intention to equalize the Bounty of ten per Cent. allowed on the Duty on Goods imported into America in American Shipping;—Additional Duties upon naval Stores, Timber, &c. would check the Importation of thofe Articles, and operate to leffen the Confumption of Britifh Manufactures in thofe Places, particularly in North Carolina, where they have fcarcely any thing elfe to pay for them;—Additional Duties in general would be a heavy Clog upon the Re-export of American Produce from Great Britain.—To meet the ten per Cent. Bounty allowed on the Duty on Goods imported into America in American Bottoms, the two following Schemes are, with all due Deference, fubmitted:

Firft—That a Duty be laid upon all Goods fhipped on board of American Veffels bound to America, equal to the ten per Cent. Bounty allowed on the Duty in America, to be paid by the Shipper of fuch Goods, whofe Correfpondent in America will have the fame allowed to him there.

Or,

Secondly—That all Goods entered outwards on board American Veffels, bound to America, be entered free of any new Duty to the Shipper of fuch
Goods;

Goods; fuch Shipper or Exporter of them, fpecifying very exactly the Con-
tents of his Entry; and in cafe they be Goods, which pay Duty *ad valorem* in
America, he to afcertain the Value of fuch Goods upon Oath; that, on
fuch American Veffel *clearing out, the Captain* fhall pay the exact Amount
of the Bounty, which will be allowed in America by the Difcount of ten
per Cent. on the Duty payable inwards; this to be paid, exclufive of the
Tonnage, to be paid as hereafter fpecified.—To meet the Tonnage Duty
impofed by the Americans, a Tonnage Duty might be impofed on American Veffels, equal to that laid extra upon Britifh Shipping by Congrefs,
fay forty-four Cents of a Dollar, which is exactly equal to Two Shillings
Sterling per Ton, and will perfectly countervail that Duty.

We may here, perhaps, be allowed, with all due Submiffion, to obferve,
that the nearer Britifh Shipping and that of the United States can be put
upon a State of Equality, the greater is the Probability that the Trade between the two Countries will be cemented by a friendly and lafting Intercourfe; and that for this purpofe, it might poffibly be found very expedient
to put the Shipping of the American States, which refort to the Britifh
Dominions in Europe, and return to the United States, upon the fame
footing as Britifh Veffels in regard to all Port Charges, whether of Light
Money, River Dues, Dockages, Pilotage, or by whatever other Name fuch
Duties or Payments are called, afked, and received by Law from Shipping,
and which the American Veffels pay at prefent in a greater Proportion,
being confidered as Foreigners; provided always, that fuch American Veffels return direct to the United States, and not, if they proceed to Ports or
Places not belonging to the American States.—Such Meafures as thefe,
we humbly prefume, might lead to a Treaty of Commerce mutually advantageous, and fecure to the Shipping Intereft of this Country the Share
it ought to enjoy in the Trade between Great Britain and the United States
of America; and we conceive, that the Americans by this means would
not be induced to carry their Produce to other Places in preference to
this Country, or to feek in foreign Countries thofe Articles of Merchandize, which they are accuftomed to procure from Great Britain.

[B 2]   A N-

ANSWER TO QUESTION IV.

WE conceive that the Acquiefcence of this Country in thofe Diftinctions, now made by Congrefs in favour of American Shipping, is no Security againft a future Increafe of the Tonnage Duty on Britifh Veffels in America: for this Tonnage Duty is impofed there, purpofely to give the Northern States a Monopoly of the carrying Trade of the Southern ones, which the prefent Duties are not fufficient to effect; and they are only preparatory to higher Duties which will inevitably be impofed, if not prevented by contravening Duties here, which alone can deter them from the Object they have in view, and is part of their Syftem to increafe their Naval Power.

ANSWER TO QUESTION V.

THE Americans, who, previous to the late Revolution, were precluded from going direct with their Tobacco and Rice to Foreign Markets, have fince been tempted to make the Experiment; but thefe Speculations have in general proved fatal Adventures, and would have been more checked ere now, had not the late diftreffing Famine in France, for a Time, caufed a brifk Demand there for all the Rice that arrived: As to Tobacco, the Quantity fent direct to Foreign Ports bears a fmall Proportion to that fent to Great Britain.

ANSWER TO QUESTION VI.

WE conceive that Britifh Ships, employed in the American Trade, do not carry American Produce to Foreign Ports in any confiderable degree; nor do they carry it in preference, unlefs from the Temptation of a much higher Freight or a better Market.

Nº V.

Report of the Merchants and Ship Owners of GLASGOW, *in Anfwer to the foregoing Queftions.*

Glafgow, 27th October, 1789.

A T a Meeting, in the City Hall, of the Merchants and Ship Owners of Glaf-gow, concerned in the Trade to the United States of America, called by public Advertifement, the Lord Provoft of Glafgow laid before the Meeting a Letter to him from William Fawkener, Efq. Secretary to the Lords of the Committee of Privy Council for Trade and Foreign Planta-tions, together with two Acts of the faid United States, impofing Duties of Impoft and Tonnage, and alfo fundry Queries for the Confideration of the faid Merchants and Ship Owners of Glafgow, to every Part of which their Lordfhips defire that full and particular Anfwers may be returned them by the faid Merchants and Ship Owners. And the Meeting having taken thefe Papers into Confideration, refolved, that Meffrs. James Ritchie, Alexander Ofwald, Henry Riddel, and Robert Findlay, Merchants in Glaf-gow, and William Fullarton, Merchant in Greenoch, be appointed a Com-mittee to prepare Anfwers to faid Queries and to report; of which Com-mittee the faid Robert Findlay to be Convener.

(Signed,) John Campbell, Junr. Provoft.

Glafgow, 26th November, 1789.

THE Committee, appointed as above, having this Day met to confider the Queries from the Lords of the Committee of Privy Council for Trade and Foreign Plantations, to the Merchants and Ship Owners of Glafgow, concerned in the Trade with the United States of America; and there being prefent Meffrs. James Ritchie, Alexander Ofwald, Henry Riddel, and Ro-

bert

bert Findlay, fundry Opinions were delivered upon the Subjects of thefe Queries; and the faid Committee refolve to fubmit thefe different Opinions to the Confideration of the whole Merchants and Ship Owners of Glafgow, concerned in the Trade to the United States of America, for their final Decifion, as to the Anfwers to be returned by them to the Lords of the Committee of Privy Council for Trade and Foreign Plantations.

(Signed,) Ro. Findlay, Convener.

Glafgow, 10th December, 1789.

AT a Meeting, in the City Hall, of the Merchants and Ship Owners concerned in the Trade to the United States of America, called by Public Advertifement, to receive the Report of their Committee, appointed on the 27th October laft, two Reports were delivered to the Meeting by faid Committee; which Reports being read and confidered, and the Queftion being put, it was refolved by a Majority, that Report, N° I., hereto annexed, be approved of by this Meeting, and tranfmitted accordingly by the Lord Provoft to William Fawkener, Efq. Secretary to the Lords of the Committee of Privy Council for Trade and Foreign Plantations: Refolved alfo, that Report, N° II., fhould likewife be tranfmitted by the Lord Provoft to the faid William Fawkener, Efq. that the Lords of the Committee of Privy Council for Trade and Foreign Plantations may have an Opportunity of judging of the different Arguments made ufe of by the Merchants and Ship Owners of this City upon the Subject of thefe Queries.

(Signed,) John Campbell, Junr. Provoft.

R E P O R T   I.

ANSWER TO QUESTION I.

NO Doubt the Merchants and Ship Owners of Great Britain, who carried on Trade to the United States of America, have fuftained a lofs in proportion to the additional Duties of Impoft and Tonnage, which were laid upon Britifh Ships, and Goods imported in them, by the different American States, more than were laid upon American Ships and Goods imported therein.

Thefe additional Duties varied in the different States, and therefore we cannot fay with precifion, what may have been the Lofs upon the whole; but, in general, there was a Difference of $1\frac{1}{4}$ to $2\frac{1}{4}$ per cent. *of Impoft*, in favour of Goods imported into the United States in American Ships.

As to the *Tonnage* Duty again, the Variation was more confiderable in many of the different States.

In Penfylvania, the Tonnage Duty on American Ships, was only about 4 d. Sterling—on Foreign Ships *in Treaty*, 8 d.—on Foreign Ships *not in Treaty*, 2 s. 1 d.

In Maryland, the Tonnage Duty on their own Ships was 8 d. Sterling—on Foreign Ships in Treaty, 1 s.—on Britifh Ships, 3 s. 6 d.;—and on other Foreign Ships not in Treaty, 1 s. 7 d.

In Virginia, the Tonnage Duty on American Ships was about 1 s. 3 d. Sterling; and on Britifh Ships it was 4 s. 6 d.

In New-York again, the Tonnage Duty on Britifh Ships was no more than 4 d. or 5 d. and on their own Ships, we believe it was the fame; though we are not certain as to this point.

Upon

Upon the whole, however, we suppose, that, *upon an Average* of all the United States, British Ships were subjected to a Duty of 2 s. to 2 s. 6 d. Sterling per Ton more than American Ships.——Say 2 s. 3 d.

As to the *degree*, therefore, that the Merchants and Ship Owners of British Ships have suffered by the Distinction of the Duties of Impost and Tonnage against them in the United States, it can be only guessed at; but it may perhaps be nearly as follows:

Suppose 600 British Ships annually employed in the Trade to and from the United States—these may be estimated at 200 Tons burden each, which is 120,000 Tons in all, and at 2 s. 3 d. per Ton is   -   -   -   -   -   -   £.13,500

Suppose again, that each of these British Ships carried, *at an Average*, £2,000 Value of Goods into the United States, this would be £1,200,000 Value of Goods, which, at 2 per cent. the Average Distinction of the Impost is   -   -   -   £ 24,000

In all   £ 37,500

Upon this Estimate, therefore, the annual Loss to the Merchants and Ship Owners of Great Britain, previous to the late Impost and Tonnage Acts of Congress, was £ 37,500; or £ 62 : 10 : 0 Sterling, upon each British Ship on every Voyage to the United States.

ANSWER TO QUESTION II.

BRITISH Ships will be upon a better footing under the late general Impost and Tonnage Acts of Congress, than they have hitherto been upon an Average in the United States; because the Comparative Duties betwixt them and American Ships are thereby reduced.

For instance, the Difference betwixt the Tonnage on American and British Ships in the United States is now only 44 cents of a Dollar, which

may

may be reckoned 2 s. Sterling per Ton; whereas formerly it was on an Average about 2 s. 3 d. per Ton, according to the Eſtimate in the Anſwer to the preceding Queſtion. Again—The Impoſt Duties on Goods imported into the United States in *all* Ships, are now the ſame, only with this Diſtinction in favour of thoſe imported in American Ships, that theſe have a Diſcount of 10 per cent. from the Amount. Theſe Impoſt Duties are various upon different Articles; but upon an Average of an aſſorted Cargo, imported into the United States, will amount to from 6 to 7¼ per cent.— and therefore, from 2-3ds to 3-4ths per cent. againſt thoſe imported in Britiſh or other Foreign Ships.

The total additional Duties to be annually paid by Britiſh more than by American Ships, and on Goods imported in the former, will therefore now ſtand as follows, according to the Eſtimate in the Anſwer to the preceding Query:

On 120,000 Tons of Britiſh Shipping, at 2 s. per Ton   -   £ 12,000

On £ 1,200,000 Value of Goods imported therein, at ¾ per cent.   -   -   -   -   -   -   £ 9,000

In all £ 21,000

The Difference therefore in favour of Britiſh Ships under the late Impoſt and Tonnage Laws of Congreſs is £ 16,000 Sterling per annum; becauſe it has been previouſly remarked, that, under the former Laws of the particular States, they paid £ 37,000 annually; whereas now, they will only pay £ 21,000, or £ 35 Sterling on each Ship on every Voyage. Now this Extra Tax or Duty upon Britiſh Ships in the United States is, in our Opirion, fully counterbalanced by the Advantages which Britiſh Ships poſſeſs over American Ships in other reſpects.

ANSWER TO QUESTION III.

THE Britiſh Shipping, notwithſtanding all the Diſadvantages under which it has laboured in America, has hitherto certainly enjoyed a very

[C]   large

large Share of the Trade of the United States fince the Peace; nor is there any juft grounds for prefent Apprehenfion, that now, when thefe Difadvantages are leffened, they will not retain an equal Share as formerly. It muft be acknowledged, however, that an Equalization of Duties of Impoft and Tonnage, to be paid by American Ships, when they come into the Ports of this Country, would be juft and right according to the Law and Cuftom of mutual Reciprocity betwixt Nations.—At fame time, we are more doubtful as to the Policy or Expediency of at once enacting fuch a retaliating or equalizing Law in this Inftance, at leaft at prefent.—The Trade to and from the United States is of very great Importance to the Navigation, to the Ship Owners, as well as to the mercantile Intereft of this Country, by reafon of the bulky Commodities which thefe States produce, and which of courfe employ, as we have already mentioned, many Britifh Ships in tranf-porting them to a Market.—Was an equalizing Law, therefore, of Impoft and Tonnage to be immediately paffed in this Country on American Ships, it is not improbable that, however contrary to the true Intereft of the United States, the American Congrefs would at its next fubfequent Meeting enact a Law, not only to impofe ftill heavier Duties upon Britifh Ships and their Cargoes, but alfo to make an invidious unfavourable Diftinction betwixt thefe and the Shipping of other Foreign Nations, for which indeed there was a large Party, even in the late Congrefs, though by the Firmnefs of the Senate, it was at laft over-ruled, and all Foreign Ships were put upon a footing.

No doubt Great Britain could again follow up and equalize, nor have the Britifh Merchants any reafon to apprehend that the Legiflature of this Country would not in all probability ultimately prevail; yet ftill this Trial of Strength or of Skill would, in the mean time, cramp the Trade betwixt this Country and the United States, and be the Caufe of continuing or keeping alive that Animofity, which has unhappily fo long prevailed, and of preventing that Return of Harmony and good Underftanding, which would be fo comfortable and fo beneficial for both.—It might alfo have a tendency to divert the Trade of the United States into other Channels more than at prefent, from whence it might not be fo eafily recovered. For all thefe

Reafons,

Reaſons, we are of opinion, that it would at preſent be rather impolitic to enact an immediate Law for equalizing the Duties on American Ships in this Country, with thoſe now paid by Britiſh Ships in the United States; eſpecially conſidering that American Ships do in fact, in common with other Foreign Ships, pay about 1 s. 9 d. per Ton in this Country, for Light Houſes and the Trinity Houſe, more than Britiſh Ships pay.

But though we are of opinion, that it would at preſent be rather impolitic to enact ſuch an equalizing Law, yet certainly theſe Extra Impoſt and Tonnage Duties on Britiſh Ships in America are a conſiderable Grievance to the Britiſh Merchants, while the American Ships pay no ſuch Extra Duties in this Country; and therefore we would, with all Submiſſion, recommend it to the Committee of Council for Trade, to uſe their Endeavours to have them removed *by Negotiation* with the American Congreſs: This would be a more amicable Mode, and in all probability more for the Commercial Intereſt of Great Britain, than by enacting an immediate retaliating Law. *If Negotiation* fails, it will then be time enough to bring forward ſuch a meaſure; and it is in the mean time proper to remark, that every additional Duty impoſed upon American Ships in the Ports of Great Britain has a Tendency moſt aſſuredly to induce the Americans, more than they now do, to carry their Produce in their own Ships to the Ports of other Countries, inſtead of bringing it into the Ports of Great Britain; and of courſe to prevent this Country from being the Depôt of the bulky Commodities of the United States.

ANSWER TO QUESTION IV.

THERE is certainly no *abſolute ſecurity* from the Nature and Circumſtances of the Trade betwixt this Country and the United States, that Congreſs will not encreaſe the Tonnage or Impoſt Duties, or perhaps both, with the view of diminiſhing the Britiſh Ships now employed in that Trade; but, as Congreſs can never be wild enough to conclude, that it is Fear, or any ſimilar motive, which induces this Country to acquieſce for the preſent

in the late Impoſt and Tonnage Duties, and as it is aſſuredly the Intereſt of
the People of the United States, eſpecially of thoſe in the Southern States, to
cultivate a Connection with Great Britain, by enjoying the Credits which its
Merchants give, and by employing its Shipping for their bulky Commodities, in rivalſhip to the American Ships belonging to the Northern or
Eaſtern States; we ſay that, for theſe Reaſons, we do not think it probable
that a Majority will be found in Congreſs to increaſe the Duties on Britiſh
Ships, ſo as to drive them out of the Trade, eſpecially, if the reconciliat-
ing mode of Negotiation is adopted, which is pointed out in the Anſwer
to the preceding Queſtion:—But, at all events, if Congreſs ſhould ever be
ſo unwiſe as to impoſe Duties with that view, Great Britain will have it
always in her power to retaliate, by equalizing ſuch Duties on American
Ships and their Cargoes in this Country, and thus ſoon check the Evil.

ANSWER TO QUESTION V.

WE do not know that American Ships at preſent *prefer* carrying Tobacco and Rice, or ſuch Produce of America, to other Countries rather
than to Great Britain: But as theſe are bulky Commodities, and cannot
ſupport the Expence of Landing, Agency, &c. in this Country, and then
reſhipping and inſuring them to the Country of ultimate Conſumpt, and
as it is not a very large Proportion of theſe American Productions, which
Great Britain and Ireland conſume, it is for theſe Reaſons extremely natural
to tranſport them direct from America to the probable Country of Conſumpt; eſpecially at a time when the Britiſh Market has a ſufficiency for
its internal uſe, and when there is no encouragement in ſuch a caſe from
the Britiſh Legiſlature to carry it to, and land it in, that Market.—It is
therefore a certain Fact, that a greater Proportion of the bulky Produce of
the United States goes direct from America to the Ports of other Countries than Great Britain in American Ships—and it will ſtill continue ſo,
unleſs ſome encouraging Meaſures are adopted for making the Ports of
Great Britain an Emporium or Depôt for ſuch bulky Produce; becauſe
every Merchant, where he legally can, will moſt undoubtedly purſue his
own

own Intereft; and it is in general his Intereft at prefent to carry the Produce of the United States to the probable Ports of Confumpt at once, inftead of depofiting it, in the firft inftance, in the Ports of Great Britain.

ANSWER TO QUESTION VI.

FOR the very fame Reafons, which are fet forth in the Anfwer to the preceding Queftion, it is moft affuredly a Fact, that even Britifh Ships carry
a greater Proportion of the bulky Produce of America, directly from thence
to the Ports of other Countries than Great Britain, and which their Owners
or Freighters think may be ultimately the Ports of Confumpt;—perhaps,
fully 2-3ds of the whole bulky Produce of America, which falls to the
Share of Britifh Ships, may be in this manner tranfported to the Ports of
other Countries. If this was not done, the Britifh Merchants could not
pretend to compete, either with the Merchants of America, or with thofe of
other Foreign Countries, in the Sale of thofe bulky Articles at fuch ultimate Ports of Confumpt.—This Neceffity of fending Britifh Ships to Foreign Ports, inftead of bringing them into Great Britain, is much regretted
by every Merchant in the Trade; but if he did not, he muft, for the Reafons above-mentioned, relinquifh the Bufinefs altogether.—The bulky Article of Tobacco alone from the United States, employs annually from 200
to 250 Ships of all Nations, of which, at leaft, three-fourths are Britifh:
And well do we remember, that, before the unhappy American War, the
Merchant, who imported Tobacco into Great Britain, although he could
not then legally carry it in the firft Inftance any where elfe, had an Allowance of 10lbs. of Tobacco per Hogfhead *free of Duty*, and had alfo an
Allowance of a Halfpenny per lb. for all damaged Tobacco cut off at the
King's Scale and burnt:—The Mafter of the Ship likewife had a fmall Allowance in name of Portage Bill, provided he made a faithful Report of his
Cargo. Thefe Allowances were a confiderable Affiftance to the Merchant,
by enabling him to tranfport his Tobacco at a fmall additional Expence to
any Foreign Market; and fuch Tranfportation gave Employment to a
Multitude of Coafting Veffels and their Seamen; but, unhappily, thefe En-
couragements

couragements are now wholly withdrawn, even although there does not now exiſt any Neceſſity of bringing this Article in the firſt Inſtance to Great Britain. The Conſequence is, of courſe, that it goes directly to the probable Port of Conſumpt, and there the Ship is again fitted out, the Seamen's Wages expended, both amounting to not leſs upon an Average than 4 to £ 500 on every Voyage, and all the Duties on Cordage, Sailcloth, Wine, Spirits, Beer, Candles, &c. in ſuch Outfit and Expenditure, not only loſt to the Revenue of this Country, but alſo the Circulation of the whole Money, and the Employment of Tradeſmen in the above Articles, are loſt to one or other of the Sea Ports of Great Britain; and, probably, likewiſe, many of the Seamen themſelves, who, by habitually navigating from one Foreign Country to another, loſe their natural Attachment to Great Britain.

N° VI.

REPORT II. *of the Merchants and Ship Owners of* GLASGOW, *in Anſwer to the foregoing Queſtions.*

ANSWER TO QUESTION I.

THE Commerce and Shipping Intereſt of this Country have certainly ſuffered by the Diſtinctions that have been hitherto made by the different Legiſlatures of the States of America, in the Duties impoſed by them on Britiſh and Foreign Goods, to the Extent of the Difference of the Duties when imported in Britiſh or American Ships; that is to ſay, the Importers of Goods in Britiſh Ships muſt ſell their Goods ſo much cheaper; and it is obvious, that the Importers will prefer American to Britiſh Ships.—The Difference of thoſe Duties have been different in the different States; but, on an Average, they may be ſuppoſed equal to two per Cent. on the firſt Coſt of the Goods —In the ſame Manner, the American

rican Ships have been enabled to serve for less Freight, or which is the same thing, to gain more than the British Ships by the Difference of the Tonnage Duties, all other Circumstances being supposed equal.—This Difference in the Tonnage Duties, has also been very different in the different States; but, on an Average, may be supposed equal to Two Shillings and Threepence per Ton.—It is supposed, there are 600 British Ships, on an Average of 200 Tons Burthen, employed in carrying the Produce of the United States to the West Indies, to our Colonies in North America, to Britain, and to all the Ports in Europe. But to illustrate what has been said in the Case of a British Ship of 200 Tons burthen trading to the States of Virginia and Maryland, and carrying their Produce to Britain, and making three Voyages in two Years, which is equal to one and a half Voyage in one Year, and supposing every Voyage she carries out £ 2,000 Sterling Value of Goods, the yearly Disadvantage of a British Ship, compared with that of an American Ship, will stand as follows:

Difference of Duty on 200 Tons, at 2 s. 3 d. is -	22	10	0
Ditto ditto on £ 2,000 Sterling, at 2 per Cent.		
as above, is - - - - -	40	0	0
	62	10	0
Add one Half for the Half-yearly Voyage - -	31	5	0
Total Difference £ 93	15	0

between a British and an American Ship, and which is equal to $6\frac{1}{4}$ per Cent. per Annum on a Ship supposed worth £ 1,500 Sterling. Such has been the State of the Trade between Britain and America since the Peace, until the late Regulations of Congress.—It has proved a very great Encouragement to American Shipping, and an equal Discouragement to British. The Number of American Ships have increased, and are increasing—Many of them built in America by Means of British Capitals, and owned by British Merchants, but navigated by American Seamen.

AN-

ANSWER TO QUESTION II.

THE Commerce and Navigation of this Country will not be on a worfe footing under the general Duties lately impofed by Congrefs, but, on the contrary, will be on a better footing; becaufe thofe Duties are in moft of the States confiderably lefs than they were formerly.—The Difference of the Tonnage Duty being now only Two Shillings per Ton, and the Duty on Goods about 7 ½ per Cent. on the Value, from which American Ships have a Difcount of 10 per Cent. equal to ¾ per Cent. on the Value of the Goods:—So that now the Difadvantage that a Britifh Ship of 200 Tons, making 3 Voyages in two Years, and carrying the fame Value of Goods, as fuppofed in the preceding Anfwer, will ftand as follows:

Difference of Duty on a Ship of 200 Tons, at 2 s. per Ton				20	0	0
Ditto ditto on £ 2,000 Sterling Value of Goods, at ¾ per Cent. - - - -				15	0	0
				35	0	0
Add one Half for the Half-yearly Voyage - -				17	10	0
			Total	£ 52	10	0

Yearly Difference between a Britifh and an American Ship, and which is equal to 3 ½ per Cent. per Annum on £ 1,500, the fuppofed Worth of the Ship as above; this is a Difference, though greatly lower than the Duties formerly impofed by the different States, which will in Time give a decided Superiority to the American Shipping; and it has been found by Experience fince the Peace, that the Shipping, employed in the Trade to the United States, has been a very bare, if not an unprofitable, Trade.—There are other Circumftances, which will contribute to the Decay of our carrying Trade, and the Diminution of our Merchants, Ships, and Seamen, and of *confequence to the Naval Power of Great Britain.*—Such as thefe; 1ft, Before the unhappy War with America, Ships built in America were held as Britifh Ships, and great Numbers of Ships were built there by the Britifh Merchants, rather than in Britain, becaufe they were much cheaper; and

it

it is believed it will be allowed, that, after long Experience and Practice, the British Merchants in general may be supposed to understand their true Interest.—Now they are restricted to build in Britain alone, and though it must be allowed that a British Ship will last longer, she is much dearer.— 2dly, British Ships are subjected to a heavy Duty on Hemp, and to Duties on Iron, Timber, Pitch, and Tar, employed in Ship-building, far exceeding those in other Parts of Europe and in America; for Instance, the Duty on Hemp imported into Britain is £ 3 : 13 : 4 Sterling per Ton : In America, Five Shillings Sterling per Ton, to take place in May 1790 ! even though she grows, and will in Time be capable of raising excellent Hemp ! It is true, similar Duties were imposed before the American War; but our Situation then in the American Trade was different from what it is now— Britain had a Monopoly of the American Trade—She must now compete, not only with America, but all Europe.——These Observations are thrown out for the Confideration of Government.

ANSWER TO QUESTION III.

IF it should be thought proper to subject Goods brought in American Ships to the Duties payable generally on Goods brought in Foreign Ships, and also to equalize the Tonnage Duties, it will be a Discouragement to American Shipping, and an Encouragement to British Shipping, to the Extent of the present Difference of the Duty, and such Measures will not prevent the same Quantity of American Produce being brought into this Country—more will be brought in British Ships—less in American Ships. ——Since the unhappy Separation of America from Britain, our Share of the Tobacco Trade must neceffarily be confined to what is wanted for the Confumption of Britain and Ireland, or for the Supply of the Ports of the Baltic, who cannot afford to be direct Importers,—the Tobacco wanted by France, Holland, and the Ports of Germany, will generally be sent directly to these Ports, their Confumption being equal to about two thirds of the whole Tobacco of the Growth of America.—The Confumption of Rice in

[D]   Britain

Britain muſt be inconſiderable: But Britain will import Tar, Pitch, Turpentine, Lumber, &c. equal to her Conſumption and no more:—Wheat
and Flour will alſo be imported, when our Ports are open.

ANSWER TO QUESTION IV.

THERE is no Security, that Congreſs will not be encouraged to increaſe
the Duties on Britiſh and other Foreign Ships.—It is probable, that they
will increaſe theſe Duties, as their Shipping increaſe, and Britiſh Capitals
can be eaſily tranſported to America for that Purpoſe.—Foreigners have no
Title to complain of what Congreſs have done or may do in this Reſpect—
they may equalize, if they think proper.—Congreſs have, in this Inſtance,
acted with true political Wiſdom, and on ſound Principles of Navigation-
Laws, and they will not be diſpoſed to alter ſo wiſe a Syſtem.

ANSWER TO QUESTIONS V. AND VI.

BOTH Britiſh and American Ships prefer carrying the Produce of America, particularly Tobacco and Rice, to the Ports of other Countries, rather
than to thoſe of Great Britain and Ireland, excepting ſo far as Tobacco and
Rice is wanted for the Conſumption of Britain and Ireland, becauſe it will
coſt Fifteen to Twenty Shillings on every Hogſhead of Tobacco which
ſhall be ſent from Britain to France, Holland or Germany, for the Conſumption of thoſe Countries; and therefore the Tobacco and Rice, wanted
by Foreign Countries, will generally be ſent directly from America to the
Countries of Conſumption. Merchants are guided by their Intereſt; and,
in a fair and lawful Trade, when they conſult their Intereſt, they beſt conſult that of the Public. An American Merchant does not purchaſe Britiſh
Manufactures, merely *becauſe they are Britiſh,* but on account they are better ſuited to the Taſte and Faſhion of America, and are better in Quality,
and cheaper.—On the other hand, he does not diſlike the Manufactures of
France, merely becauſe they are *French,* but on account of their being
worſe

worfe in Quality and dearer, and lefs fuited to the Tafte and Fafhion of America.

It is very true, that fince the Peace, more Tobacco has been imported into Britain than was neceffary for the Confumption of Britain and Ireland : This has probably arifen from former Habits, and from an Allowance of Ten Pounds of Tobacco free of Duty on every Hogfhead of Tobacco, which was equal, at the prefent Duties, to Twelve Shillings and Sixpence Sterling per Hogfhead; and which was a Bounty granted when it was un-neceffary, perhaps improper, and has been withdrawn about four Years ago :—But it is probable, that the Importation into Britain will be dimi-nifhed nearly to the Extent of the Britifh and Irifh Confumption, and what may be wanted for the Ports in the Baltic, who cannot afford to be direct Importers.

It is obvious, that a Merchant, who imports Tobacco into Britain, and afterwards fends it to Holland, cannot carry on that Trade in Competition with a Merchant who fends Tobacco directly from America to Holland, becaufe it will coft from Fifteen to Twenty Shillings per Hogfhead, as has been already ftated, in Landing and Re-fhipping Charges, Freight, and Infurance to Holland.

(B.)

List of such Vessels (and the respective Tonnage of each Denomination) as entered the Port of Philadelphia from the 1st Day of September 1772, to the 1st Day of September 1775, distinguishing each Year; and also distinguishing those which were owned in Great Britain, Ireland, and such Parts of the British Dominions as are not now comprehended within the United States, (Nº I.); those which were owned in the Port of Philadelphia alone, (Nº II.); and those which were owned in the Thirteen Colonies which now compose the United States of America, (Nº III.).

Nº I. BRITISH.

No.	1772 to 1773.	Tons.	No.	1773 to 1774.	Tons.	No.	1774 to 1775.	Tons.
23	Ships -	3,508	28	Ships -	4,304	35	Ships -	5,590
30	Brigantines	2,925	33	Brigantines	2,853	33	Brigantines	3,170
4	Snows -	370	12	Snows -	1,246	7	Snows -	730
22	Sloops -	1,043	24	Sloops -	1,142	22	Sloops -	1,006
18	Schooners -	822	22	Schooners -	962	17	Schooners -	842
97		8,668	119		10,507	114		11,338

Nº II. PHILADELPHIA.

No.	1772 to 1773.	Tons.	No.	1773 to 1774.	Tons.	No.	1774 to 1775.	Tons.
109	Ships -	16,385	116	Ships -	17,569	146	Ships -	23,406
140	Brigantines	12,148	176	Brigantines	15,749	205	Brigantines	17,802
25	Snows -	2,902	18	Snows -	2,092	17	Snows -	1,972
39	Sloops -	1,806	42	Sloops -	1,844	36	Sloops -	1,844
63	Schooners	3,226	54	Schooners	2,959	35	Schooners	1,834
376		36,467	406		40,213	439		46,858

Nº III. AMERICA.

No.	1772 to 1773.	Tons.	No.	1773 to 1774.	Tons.	No.	1774 to 1775.	Tons.
5	Ships -	700	6	Ships -	860	7	Ships -	902
46	Brigantines	3,856	28	Brigantines	2,224	30	Brigantines	2,576
1	Snow -	160				1	Snow -	80
139	Sloops -	6,503	135	Sloops -	5,876	130	Sloops -	5,843
80	Schooners -	3,899	81	Schooners	3,962	78	Schooners -	4,025
271		15,118	250		12,922	246		13,426

A Table shewing what Proportion the Tonnage of Great Britain employed out of the Port of Philadelphia bore to the Tonnage employed out of that Port, and owned therein, upon an Average of Three Years antecedent to the War; and what Proportion the Tonnage of Great Britain so employed then bore to the Tonnage of Philadelphia, united with the Tonnage of the other Twelve American Colonies so employed.

Shewing also, what Proportion the British Tonnage now employed in the Trade of Philadelphia bears to the Tonnage of all the United States employed out of that Port, upon an Average of the last Two Years.

	1773.	1774.	1775.	Total.
	Tons.	Tons.	Tons.	Tons.
British - -	8,668	10,507	11,333	30,508
Philadelphia - -	36,467	40,213	46,858	123,538
American - -	15,118	12,922	13,426	41,466
Philadelphia and America combined -	51,583	53,135	60,284	165,004

By the foregoing Table it appears, that the Tonnage of Great Britain employed out of the Port of Philadelphia in the above Years was not equal to 1-4th Part of the Tonnage employed out of and owned in the Port of Philadelphia;—and that the Tonnage of Great Britain then so employed, bore only a Proportion as 2 does to 11 to the Tonnage of Philadelphia and the other Twelve Colonies combined so employed.

	1788.	1789.	Total.
	Tons.	Tons.	Tons.
British -	23,004	29,372	52,376
American -	28,028	37,728	65,756

By the above Table it appears, that the Tonnage of Great Britain employed out of the Port of Philadelphia in the Years 1788 and 1789, amounted to within 1 5th Part of the Tonnage of all the Thirteen United States combined so employed.

A Lift of Britiſh Veſſels which entered the Port of Philadelphia the following Years, viz. from 5 September 1787, to 5 September 1788.

From Great Britain.		Ireland.		Britiſh Weſt Indies.		Britiſh American Colonies.	
Veſſels.	Tons.	Veſſels.	Tons.	Veſſels.	Tons.	Veſſels.	Tons.
16 Ships -	3,748	4 Ships -	1,021	1 Ship -	174		
19 Brigantines	2,907	1 Brig -	135	52 Brigs -	6,229	1 Ship -	160
3 Snows -	456	1 Snow -	90	64 Sloops -	5,597	6 Brigantines	462
3 Sloops -	198			24 Schooners	1,695	1 Schooner -	47
1 Schooner -	85						
42 Sail.	7,394	6 Sail.	1,246	141 Sail.	13,695	8 Sail.	669

Total.

22 Ships
78 Brigantines
4 Snows   } 197 Sail Veſſels — 23,004 Tons.
67 Sloops
26 Schooners

Ditto, from 5 September 1788, to 5 September 1789.

From Great Britain.		Ireland.		Britiſh Weſt Indies.		Britiſh American Colonies.	
Veſſels.	Tons.	Veſſels.	Tons.	Veſſels.	Tons.	Veſſels.	Tons.
23 Ships -	5,967	15 Ships -	2,961	3 Ships -	600		
19 Brigantines	2,936	5 Brigantines	631	48 Brigantines	6,010	1 Ship -	162
1 Snow -	104	1 Snow -	108	69 Sloops -	5,586	10 Brigantines	1,060
4 Sloops -	223			29 Schooners	2,332	2 Sloops -	106
1 Schooner -	42					7 Schooners -	544
48 Sail.	9,272	21 Sail.	3,700	149 Sail.	14,528	20 Sail.	1,872

Total.

42 Ships
82 Brigantines
2 Snows   } 238 Sail Veſſels — 29,372 Tons.
75 Sloops
37 Schooners

(C.)

An ACT *for laying a* DUTY *on* GOODS, WARES, *and* MERCHAN-
DIZES *imported into the* UNITED STATES.

[Repealed by Seff. 2. ch. 39. New Duties to commence 1 Jan. 1791.]

SECTION I. WHEREAS it is neceffary for the fupport of government, for the difcharge of the debts of the United States, and the encouragement and protection of manufactures, that duties be laid on goods, wares, and merchandizes imported,

Be it enacted by the SENATE *and* HOUSE *of* REPRESENTATIVES *of the United States of America in Congrefs affembled,* That from and after the firft day of Auguft next enfuing, the feveral duties herein after mentioned fhall be laid on the following goods, wares and merchandizes imported into the United States, from any foreign port or place, that is to fay :

On all diftilled fpirits of Jamaica proof, imported from any kingdom or country whatfoever, - - - per gallon, ten cents.
On all other diftilled fpirits, - - per gallon, eight cents.
On molaffes, - - per gallon, two and a half cents.
On Madeira wine, - - per gallon, eighteen cents.
On all other wines, - - per gallon, ten cents.
On every gallon of beer, ale or porter in cafks, - five cents.
On all cyder, beer, ale or porter in bottles, per dozen, - five cents.
On malt, - - · - per bufhel, ten cents.
On brown fugars, - - - per pound, one cent.
On loaf fugars, - - - per pound, three cents.
On all other fugars, - - per pound, one and a half cents.
On coffee, - - per pound, two and a half cents.
On cocoa, - - - per pound, one cent.

On

On all candles of tallow,   -   -   per pound, two cents.
On all candles of wax or fpermaceti,   -   per pound, fix cents.
On cheefe,   -   -   -   per pound, four cents.
On foap,   -   -   -   per pound, two cents.
On boots,   -   -   -   per pair, fifty cents.
On all fhoes, flippers, or golofhoes, made of leather,
     per pair,   -   -   -   -   feven cents.
On all fhoes or flippers made of filk or ftuff, per pair,   ten cents.
On cables, for every one hundred and twelve pounds, feventy-five cents.
On tarred cordage, for every one hundred and twelve
     pounds,   -   -   -   -   feventy-five cents.
On untarred ditto, and yarn, for every one hundred
     and twelve pounds,   -   -   -   -   ninety cents,
On twine or packthread, for every one hundred and
     twelve pounds,   -   -   -   two hundred cents.
On all fteel unwrought, for every one hundred and
     twelve pounds,   -   -   -   fifty-fix cents.
On all nails and fpikes,   -   -   per pound, one cent.
On falt,   -   -   -   -   per bufhel, fix cents.
On manufactured tobacco,   -   -   per pound, fix cents.
On fnuff,   -   -   -   per pound, ten cents.
On indigo,   -   -   -   per pound, fixteen cents.
On wool and cotton cards,   -   per dozen, fifty cents.
On coal,   -   -   -   per bufhel, two cents.
On pickled fifh,   -   -   per barrel, feventy-five cents.
On dried fifh,   -   -   -   per quintal, fifty cents.

On all teas imported from China or India in fhips built in the United States,
and belonging to a citizen or citizens thereof, or in fhips or veffels built ·
in foreign countries, and on the fixteenth day of May laft wholly the
property of a citizen or citizens of the United States, and fo continuing
until the time of importation, as follows :

On

On bohea tea,   -   -   -   per pound, fix cents.
On all fouchong, or other black teas,   -   per pound, ten cents.
On all hyfon teas   -   -   -   per pound, twenty cents.
On all other green teas,   -   -   per pound, twelve cents.

On all teas imported from Europe in fhips or veffels built in the United
    States, and belonging wholly to a citizen or citizens thereof, or in fhips
    or veffels built in foreign countries, and on the fixteenth day of May laft
    wholly the property of a citizen or citizens of the United States, and fo
    continuing until the time of importation, as follows :

On bohea tea,   -   -   -   per pound, eight cents.
On all fouchong, and other black teas,   per pound, thirteen cents.
On all hyfon teas,   -   -   per pound, twenty-fix cents.
On all other green teas,   -   -   per pound, fixteen cents.

On all teas imported in any other manner than as abovementioned, as
    follows :

On bohea tea,   -   -   -   per pound, fifteen cents.
On all fouchong, or other black teas,   per pound, twenty-two cents.
On all hyfon teas,   -   -   per pound, forty-five cents.
On all other green teas,   -   per pound, twenty-feven cents.

On all goods, wares and merchandizes, other than teas, imported from
    China or India, in fhips not built in the United States, and not wholly
    the property of a citizen or citizens thereof, nor in veffels built in foreign
    countries, and on the fixteenth day of May laft wholly the property of a
    citizen or citizens of the United States, and fo continuing until the time
    of importation, twelve and a half per centum ad valorem.

On all looking-glaffes, window and other glafs ⎫
    (except black quart bottles)   ⎪
On all China, ftone and earthen ware   ⎬ ten per centum ad valorem.
On gun-powder   -   -   -   - ⎭

[E]   On

On all paints ground in oil,   -   -
On fhoe and knee buckles,   -   -
On gold and filver lace, and
On gold and filver leaf   -   -
} ten per centum ad valorem.

On all blank books,   -   -   -   -
On all writing, printing, or wrapping paper, paper hangings, and
    pafteboard,   -   -   -   -
On all cabinet wares,   -   -   -   -
On all buttons,   -   -   -   -   -
On all faddles,   -   -   -   -
On all gloves of leather,   -   -   -   -
On all hats of beaver, fur, wool, or mixture of either,   -
On all millenary ready made,   -   -   -
On all caftings of iron, and upon flit and rolled iron,   -
On all leather tanned or tawed, and all manufacture of leather, except
    fuch as fhall be otherwife rated,   -   -   -
On canes, walking fticks and whips,   -   -
On cloathing ready made,   -   -   -
On all brufhes,   -   -   -   -   -
On gold, filver and plated ware, and on jewellery and pafte work,
On anchors, and on all wrought tin and pewter ware,   -
} Seven and an half per centum ad valorem.

On playing cards,   -   -   -   per pack, ten cents.

On every coach, chariot, or other four wheel
    carriage, and on every chaife, folo, or other
    two wheel carriage, or parts thereof,   -
} fifteen per centum ad valorem.

On all other goods, wares and merchandize, five per centum on the value thereof, at the time and place of importation, except as follows: Salt-
petre, tin in pigs, tin-plates, lead, old pewter, brafs, iron and brafs wire,
copper in plates, wool, cotton, dying woods and dying drugs, raw hides,
beaver, and all other furs and deer-fkins.

SEC. 2. *And be it further enacted by the authority aforefaid,* That from
and after the firft day of December which fhall be in the year one thoufand

                                                         feven

feven hundred and ninety, there fhall be laid a duty on every one hundred and twelve pounds weight of hemp imported as aforefaid, of fixty cents; and on cotton per pound three cents.

SEC. 3. *And be it enacted by the authority aforefaid,* That all the duties paid, or fecured to be paid upon any of the goods, wares, and merchandizes as aforefaid, except on diftilled fpirits, other than brandy and geneva, fhall be returned or difcharged upon fuch of the faid goods, wares or merchandizes, as fhall within twelve months after payment made, or fecurity given, be exported to any country, without the limits of the United States, as fettled by the late treaty of peace; except one per centum on the amount of the faid duties, in confideration of the expence which fhall have accrued by the entry and fafe-keeping thereof.

SEC. 4. *And be it enacted by the authority aforefaid,* That there fhall be allowed and paid on every quintal of dried, and on every barrel of pickled fifh, of the fifheries of the United States, and on every barrel of falted provifion of the United States, exported to any country without the limits thereof, in lieu of a drawback of the duties impofed on the importation of the falt employed and expended therein, viz.

On every quintal of dried fifh,	-	-	-	five cents.
On every barrel of pickled fifh,	-	-	-	five cents.
On every barrel of falted provifion,		-	-	five cents.

SEC. 5. *And be it further enacted by the authority aforefaid,* That a difcount of ten per cent. on all the duties impofed by this act, fhall be allowed on fuch goods, wares and merchandizes, as fhall be imported in veffels built in the United States, and which fhall be wholly the property of a citizen or citizens thereof, or in veffels built in foreign countries, and on the fixteenth day of May laft wholly the property of a citizen or citizens of the United States, and fo continuing until the time of importation.

SEC. 6. *And be it further enacted by the authority aforefaid,* That this act fhall continue and be in force until the firft day of June which fhall be in

the

the year of our Lord one thoufand feven hundred and ninety-fix, and from thence until the end of the next fucceeding feffion of Congrefs, which fhall be held thereafter, and no longer.

FREDERICK AUGUSTUS MUHLENBERG,
Speaker of the Houfe of Reprefentatives.

JOHN ADAMS, *Vice Prefident of the United States,*
and Prefident of the Senate.

APPROVED, JUNE 1, 1789.

GEORGE WASHINGTON, *Prefident of the United States.*

(D.)

An ACT *making further Provifion for the* PAYMENT *of the* DEBTS *of the* UNITED STATES.

WHEREAS, by an act, intituled, " An act for laying a duty on goods, wares and merchandizes imported into the United States," divers duties were laid on goods, wares and merchandize fo imported, for the difcharge of the debts of the United States, and the encouragement and protection of manufactures: And whereas the fupport of government and the difcharge of the faid debts, render it neceffary to encreafe the faid duties:

SEC. I. *Be it enacted by the* SENATE *and* HOUSE *of* REPRESENTATIVES *of the United States of America in Congrefs affembled,* That from and after the laft day of December next, the duties fpecified and laid in and by the act aforefaid, fhall ceafe and determine; and that upon all goods, wares and merchandize (not herein particularly excepted) which after the faid day fhall be brought into the United States, from any foreign port or place, there fhall be levied, collected and paid the feveral and refpective duties following, that is to fay: Madeira wine of the quality of London particular, per gallon, thirty-five cents; other Madeira wine, per gallon, thirty cents; Sherry wine, per gallon, twenty-five cents; other wines, per gallon, twenty cents; diftilled fpirits, if more than ten per cent. below proof, according to Dycas's hydrometer, per gallon, twelve cents; if more than five, and not more than ten per cent. below proof, according to the fame hydrometer, per gallon, twelve and an half cents; if of proof, and not more than five per cent. below proof, according to the fame hydrometer, per gallon, thirteen cents; if above proof, but not exceeding twenty per cent. according to the fame hydrometer, per gallon, fifteen cents; if of more than twenty, and not more than forty per cent. above proof, according to the fame hydrometer, per gallon, twenty cents; if of more than forty per cent. above proof, according

cording to the fame hydrometer, per gallon, twenty-five cents; molaffes, per gallon, three cents; beer, ale and porter in cafks, per gallon, five cents; beer, ale and porter in bottles, per dozen, twenty cents. Teas from China and India, in fhips or veffels of the United States, bohea, per pound, ten cents; fouchong and other black teas, per pound, eighteen cents; hyfon, per pound, thirty-two cents; other green teas, per pound, twenty cents: Teas from Europe, in fhips or veffels of the United States; bohea, per pound, twelve cents; fouchong and other black teas, per pound, twenty-one cents; hyfon, per pound, forty cents; other green teas, per pound, twenty-four cents: Teas from any other place, or in any other fhips or vef-fels, bohea per pound, fifteen cents; fouchong and other black teas per pound, twenty-feven cents; hyfon per pound, fifty cents; other green teas per pound, thirty cents; coffee per pound, four cents; cocoa per pound, one cent; loaf fugar per pound, five cents; brown fugar per pound, one and an half cent; other fugar per pound, two and an half cents; candles of tallow per pound, two cents; candles of wax or fpermaceti per pound, fix cents; cheefe per pound, four cents; foap per pound, two cents; pepper per pound, fix cents; pimento per pound, four cents; manufactured to-bacco per pound, fix cents; fnuff per pound, ten cents; indigo per pound, twenty-five cents; cotton per pound, three cents; nails and fpikes per pound, one cent; barr and other lead per pound, one cent; fteel unwrought per one hundred and twelve pounds, feventy-five cents; hemp per one hundred and twelve pounds, fifty-four cents; cables per one hundred and twelve pounds, one hundred cents; tarred cordage per one hundred and twelve pounds, one hundred cents; untarred cordage and yarn per one hundred and twelve pounds, one hundred and fifty cents; twine and packthread per one hundred and twelve pounds, three hundred cents; falt per bufhel, twelve cents; malt per bufhel, ten cents; coal per bufhel, three cents; boots per pair, fifty cents; fhoes, flippers and golofhoes, made of leather, per pair, feven cents; fhoes and flippers made of filk or ftuff, per pair, ten cents; wool and cotton cards, per dozen, fifty cents; playing cards, per pack, ten cents; all china ware, looking glaffes, window and other glafs, and all manufactures of glafs, (black quart bottles excepted,) twelve and an half per centum ad valorem; marble, flate and other ftones, bricks, tiles,

cables,

cables, mortars and other utenfils of marble or flate, and generally all ftone and earthen ware, blank books, writing paper, and wrapping paper, paper hangings, pafte-boards, parchment and vellum, pictures and prints, painters colors, including lampblack, except thofe commonly ufed in dying, gold, filver and plated ware, gold and filver lace, jewellery and pafte work, clocks and watches, fhoe and knee buckles, grocery, (except the articles before enumerated,) namely, cinnamon, cloves, mace, nutmegs, ginger, annifeed, currants, dates, figs, plumbs, prunes, raifins, fugar-candy, oranges, lemons, limes, and generally, all fruits and comfits, olives, capers and pickles of every fort, oil, gun-powder, muftard in flour, ten per centum ad valorem; cabinet-wares, buttons, faddles, gloves of leather, hats of beaver, felt, wool, or a mixture of any of them, millenary ready made, caftings of iron, and flit and rolled iron, leather tanned or tawed, and all manufactures of which leather is the article of chief value, except fuch as are herein otherwife rated, canes, walking-fticks and whips, cloathing ready made, brufhes, anchors, all wares of tin, pewter, or copper, all or any of them, medicinal drugs, except thofe commonly ufed in dying, carpets and carpeting, all velvets, velverets, fattins and other wrought filks, cambrics, muflins, muflinets, lawns, laces, gauzes, chintzes, and colored callicoes, and nankeens, feven and an half per centum ad valorem. All goods, wares and merchandize imported directly from China or India in fhips or veffels not of the United States, teas excepted, twelve and an half per centum ad valorem. All coaches, chariots, phaetons, chaifes, chairs, folos or other carriages, or parts of carriages, fifteen and an half per centum ad valorem; and five per centum ad valorem upon all other goods, wares and merchandize, except bullion, tin in pigs, tin plates, old pewter, brafs teutenague, iron and brafs wire, copper in plates, falt petre, plaifter of Paris, wool, dying woods, and dying drugs, raw hides and fkins, undreffed furrs of every kind, the fea-ftores of fhips or veffels, the cloaths, books, houfhold furniture, and the tools or implements of the trade or profeffion of perfons who come to refide in the United States, philofophical apparatus fpecially imported for any feminary of learning, all goods intended to be re-exported to a foreign port or place, in the fame fhip or veffel in which they fhall be imported, and generally, all articles of the growth, product or manufactures of the United States.

SEC.

SEC. 2. *And be it further enacted*, That an addition of ten per centum shall be made to the several rates of duties above specified and imposed, in respect to all goods, wares and merchandize, which, after the said last day of December next, shall be imported in ships or vessels not of the United States, except in the cases in which an additional duty is herein before specially laid on any goods, wares or merchandizes, which shall be imported in such ships or vessels.

SEC. 3. *And be it further enacted*, That all duties which shall be paid or secured to be paid by virtue of this act, shall be returned or discharged in respect to all such goods, wares or merchandize, whereupon they shall have been so paid, or secured to be paid, as, within twelve calendar months after payment made or security given, shall be exported to any foreign port or place, except one per centum on the amount of the said duties, which shall be retained as an indemnification for whatever expense may have accrued concerning the same.

SEC. 4. *And be it further enacted*, That there shall be allowed and paid on dried and pickled fish, of the fisheries of the United States, and on other provisions salted within the said States, which after the said last day of December next, shall be exported therefrom to any foreign port or place, in lieu of a drawback of the duty on the salt which shall have been expended thereupon, according to the following rates, namely, dried fish per quintal, ten cents, pickled fish and other salted provisions, per barrel, ten cents.

SEC. 5. *And be it further enacted*, That where duties by this act are imposed, or drawbacks allowed on any specific quantity of goods, wares and merchandize, the same shall be deemed to apply in proportion to any quantity, more or less, than such specific quantity.

SEC. 6. *And be it further enacted*, That all the duties which by virtue of the act intituled, " An act for laying a duty on goods, wares and merchandizes imported into the United States," accrued between the time specified in the said act for the commencement of the said duties, and the respective times
when

when the collectors entered upon the duties of their respective offices in the several districts, be, and they are hereby remitted and discharged, and that in any case in which they may have been paid to the United States, restitution thereof shall be made.

SEC. 7. *And be it further enacted,* That the several duties imposed by this act shall continue to be collected and paid, until the debts and purposes, for which they are pledged and appropriated, shall be fully discharged. *Provided,* that nothing herein contained shall be construed to prevent the legislature of the United States from substituting other duties or taxes of equal value to any or all of the said duties and imposts.

FREDERICK AUGUSTUS MUHLENBERG,
Speaker of the House of Representatives.

JOHN ADAMS, *Vice-President of the United States,*
and President of the Senate.

APPROVED, August the tenth, 1790.
GEORGE WASHINGTON, *President of the United States.*

For EU product safety concerns, contact us at Calle de José Abascal, 56–1°,
28003 Madrid, Spain or eugpsr@cambridge.org.

www.ingramcontent.com/pod-product-compliance
Ingram Content Group UK Ltd.
Pitfield, Milton Keynes, MK11 3LW, UK
UKHW030902150625
459647UK00021B/2668